REINCARNATION

For Robert Coppola —
One of the kindest
people I have the
pleasure to know.

Donald Nevins

6 May, 1999
(Nicholas's Birthday)

REINCARNATION

AMAZING TRUE CASES FROM AROUND THE WORLD

ROY STEMMAN

PIATKUS

Cover photograph information: *left* The Seventeenth Karmapa of Tibet (see Chapter 8); *centre* The Giza Pyramids, Egypt; *right* Irishwoman Mary Sutton with her daughter Phyllis in 1927 (see Chapter 2, pages 18–9, for the case of Jenny Cockell who believes she was Mary Sutton in a past life).

© 1997 Roy Stemman

First published in 1997 by
Judy Piatkus (Publishers) Ltd
5 Windmill Street, London W1P 1HF

This paperback edition published
in 1998

**The moral right of the author
has been asserted**

*A catalogue record for this book is available
from the British Library*

ISBN 0–7499–1708–3 hbk
ISBN 0–7499–1787–3 pbk

Data capture & manipulation by
Action Typesetting Limited, Gloucester
Printed and bound in Great Britain by
Mackays of Chatham PLC, Chatham, Kent

CONTENTS

ACKNOWLEDGEMENTS

No book which examines the scientific evidence for reincarnation could be written without reference to the work of Professor Ian Stevenson, and mine is no exception. He is the world's foremost expert on reincarnation and, like other writers on the subject, I owe him an enormous debt of gratitude for his pioneering and painstaking research. Canadian-born Ian Stevenson is Carlson Professor of Psychiatry at the University of Virginia, USA, where he is also Director of the Division of Personality Studies of the Department of Behavioural Medicine and Psychiatry. He has spent many years investigating the very best cases from around the world and I have drawn extensively on his published research (see Bibliography). Although his studies have attracted some criticism, this has not changed my own view that his work, and that of others, provides a formidable body of evidence for the concept of rebirth and has also contributed greatly to our knowledge of man's spiritual dimension.

There are many others working in the field whose efforts I admire and whose co-operation I value. Most of those mentioned here have been supportive of *Reincarnation International Magazine*, which I edit, and whose files form the basis of much that is in these pages. Joe Fisher in Canada, Ian Wilson in New Zealand, Rabbi Yonassan Gershom in the USA, Gaj Raj Gaur in India, Hernani Guimarães Andrade in Brazil and Professor Erlendur Haraldsson in Iceland are among the magazine's correspondents, and I am delighted to acknowledge their contributions to this book.

Others who have written or supplied material, for no other motive than to share evidence for reincarnation with others, include Guy Lyon Playfair (whose translation and excellent review of Andrade's book on Father Jonathan is quoted at length in Chapter 16) and Colin Wilson. David Christie-Murray, whose scholarly book on reincarnation is the one I most often recommend to enquirers (see Bibliography), is another of our regular contributors, as is Gladys Archer, who supplied much of the material on the case of Captain Arthur Flowerdew (Chapter 19). My good friend Tom Barlow, a hypnotist and researcher, has been supportive throughout the project and given valuable assistance in a number of ways. Bob, Peter and Carl Hulme have diligently kept me informed of their progress as they research the life of John Rafael (Chapter 19).

Gaj Raj Gaur deserves a special mention for travelling overnight to meet me during my brief visit to Delhi in 1994 and subsequently providing me with many new cases of children remembering past lives, particularly those featuring birthmarks or birth defects. No one has done more than Joe Keeton to research the power of the mind and the ability to recall past lives under hypnosis. His wife, Monica O'Hara-Keeton, is now making her own important contribution with a detailed study of her own previous life. I am grateful to both of them for their encouragement.

My son Paul has also been a great help, not only editorially but also with the computer technology which plays such a vital role in publishing today. When I have been unable to solve a technical problem he has always been ready to come to the rescue.

Finally, it would not have been possible for me to write *Reincarnation* without the support of Danny Lee who, as well as being the administrative backbone of *Reincarnation International Magazine*, has also acted as my researcher and proof-reader on this book, both of which tasks made demands upon his time which went far beyond the call of duty.

To everyone I have mentioned, and to the many more who have also helped me put the evidence for reincarnation before a wider audience, I am deeply grateful.

INTRODUCTION

I t was a teacher of religious education who was probably responsible for my fascination with life after death ... but for all the wrong reasons. He was the Rev. E.G. Taylor, a large, jolly man with crew-cut hair and craggy features, who taught at the North London school I attended. During his divinity lessons our minds tended to wander but there was one aspect which always intrigued me. He became particularly animated when he discussed miracles and would regale us with stories like the Crossing of the Red Sea and Moses and the Burning Bush, then offer us perfectly normal explanations for these apparently miraculous events. There would have been a certain time of day, he suggested, at which someone who knew about tides could lead a large number of people across this stretch of water and a pursuing army would become engulfed in the rising waters. Moses' 'trick' with the burning bush was similarly explained in terms of a natural phenomenon.

I have never looked into these hypotheses to see if he was right or wrong. What fascinated me, however, was that a priest should be arguing *against* divine intervention in these and other biblical accounts. Indeed, he seemed largely sceptical of all things miraculous, and would have made an ideal member of one of the many sceptics' associations which seem to be in vogue at present. Being young and curious, his approach only increased my interest in so-called 'miracles'. Before long I was an avid reader of books about psychical research, Spiritualism, reincarnation and associated subjects.

It was but a small step from being absorbed, confused and fascinated by such third-hand accounts of life after death to deciding that I needed to find out for myself whether the so-called 'dead' really did survive the grave and could communicate with us. That decision took me, as an adult, to a leafy suburban street in Golders Green, north-west London, to the home of a veteran medium, Mrs Bertha Harris. It was my tremendous good fortune to have my first sitting with someone who, I now realise, was an extremely good medium – an experience that is, I fear, all too rare nowadays.

Being of a sceptical frame of mind, I was determined to do and say as little as possible that might provide Mrs Harris with clues. I took the precaution of booking the sitting under a different name and answered only 'yes' or 'no' to the few questions she asked during the two-hour session. As well as a wealth of personal information about which she could not possibly have known, even had I supplied her with my real name before that meeting, she also told me that her spirit helpers were telling her something which I could not possibly have known myself. They explained that I was very sceptical and that afterwards I might well explain away what she had told me as 'reading my mind'.

She then proceeded to describe the office in which I worked and said, correctly, that I worked with a number of others in that office but only one was a man. This man was my boss but not *the* boss. Mrs Harris was aware of the spirit presence of a man who was the father of this person she had identified. 'He tells me his name is Smith,' she continued. 'I'm sorry that it's such a common name, but I can't change it. He says his initials are W.G. or W.J., I'm having trouble hearing whether it's a G or J, and he died of a lung condition. You know nothing about this and will have to check it.'

I was convinced she was wrong. It was true that the assistant editor on the trade journal on which I then worked was named Arthur Smith, but he had often talked about visiting his parents at the weekend. So I was certain that his father was very much alive. Nevertheless, it was important, in order to judge Mrs Harris and the spirit hypothesis fairly, for me to check the facts. The opportunity came over lunch during our weekly visit to the printer. Arthur, a tall, thin pipe-smoker in his mid-forties, was rather taken aback by my question, since until that moment he had no idea that I had an interest in spiritualism.

His father's initials and cause of death were written on a piece of paper which I had placed in my pocket that morning and I now produced it, together with my explanation.

'My father is dead,' he confirmed. 'He died when I was about four years old and my mother remarried. His initials were W.G. but I don't know what the cause of his death was. I believe he suffered an injury to his side from which he never recovered. But I'm seeing my mother this weekend – I'll ask her.'

He did, and revealed on the following Monday that his father *had* died from a lung condition, as Bertha Harris had told me, caused by inhaling mustard gas during the First World War.

This story may not convince the sceptics but, taken together with all the other information I had been given, it satisfied me that some part of our consciousness does survive death and can communicate with this world under certain circumstances – such as when there is a gifted medium to act as a go-between. During eight years as assistant editor of *Psychic News*, a weekly Spiritualist newspaper, I received even more survival evidence, but never anything to better that very first sitting.

Continuing my quest for satisfactory evidence for life after death, I discovered that accounts of the next world communicated through mediums by spirit guides and others were sometimes contradictory. Their descriptions differed. Their beliefs clashed. Even their views on God, Jesus and other religious figures did not always agree.

In fact, seen from another perspective, these differences are not so surprising. If aliens landed six spaceships at six different points on Earth and then returned home with separate accounts of their encounters, their fellow beings might well wonder whether they had been to the same planet. One alien team would describe a world in which snow and ice covered the ground and the inhabitants were clothed in fur to keep out the freezing cold. Another group would tell of black-skinned people living in searing temperatures and wearing very little.

Yet another would describe very tall buildings in which people of various-coloured skins lived and where they travelled around in vehicles. Each would be telling the truth, of course, and the same may be true of the spirit guides who attempt to describe the next world.

But the disagreement over whether we are reborn or not is more puzzling and so I began to make a detailed study of the evidence for reincarnation. I knew, of course, that Buddhists and Hindus believed we lived earthly lives but it came as a surprise to discover just how ancient a belief it was. There are teachings going back 5,000 years and Hinduism, which began about that time, was also the first religion to incorporate reincarnation into its basic tenets. There's even evidence that it was embraced by the early Christians before being declared 'anathema' in AD 553. It's to be found in Jainism and Sikhism, in some factions of the Jewish faith, and in the native faiths of many peoples around the world. In Africa, alone, for example, it is said that thirty-six tribes believe in human reincarnation and a further eleven believe in rebirth as animals. What this means is that well over half our planet's population believe that we are reborn, time and again.

I then discovered that, despite this global leaning towards a belief in reincarnation, the idea is shunned by large numbers of Spiritualists in America and Britain. There are many well-known spirit guides who have said they know of no cases of rebirth. Prominent Spiritualists who follow these guides' teachings argue that we live just one life on earth and then spend eternity in the spirit world. But in France and other parts of Europe, as well as in South America, Spiritists – who follow the teachings of Allan Kardec, based on the thousands of spirit messages he received at the end of the nineteenth century through many mediums – are strong believers in reincarnation.

The lesson I learned from my own study of these other-world accounts is not to regard any one spiritual source as 'gospel'. There is probably truth in each. The last thing we should do is to allow such spirit messages to make us narrow-minded or bigoted. I also found the concept of a next world in which the sun always shines and flowers always bloom – often referred to as 'the Summerland' – too good to be true.

The rough and tumble of a life on earth, with all its excitements and pitfalls, seems to be a valuable 'classroom' for us to learn lessons, and it also seems logical that we might have to pass through many classrooms before we are ready to graduate.

Just as the apparent conflict in the beliefs of my divinity teacher inspired me to make my own investigation of spiritual matters, so this vital difference of opinion about the nature of our continuing life after death has also focused my own interest in the area of reincarnation.

For more than thirty years I have been collecting testimonies from people who believe they have lived on earth before, in another body, and I have come to realise that there is a large and impressive body of evidence which supports the view that these are very real experiences and not fantasy. In this book, I share just a few of the thousands of case studies on record which have particularly impressed me. Since launching my own publication, *Reincarnation International Magazine*, in 1993, I have begun to receive reports from people who believe they have strong evidence to support their claims of remembering past lives. I hope this book will also inspire some readers to share their experiences with me.

On a deeper level, I believe reincarnation offers us an explanation for the apparent unfairness of life. It allows for the possibility that the rich man in this life will be poor in the next, and vice versa. It puts our ills, misfortunes, premature death or long-term suffering in context, not as accidents of birth but as episodes in a grand scheme in which the law of cause and effect – karma – ensures that the balance will always be restored and that there will always be opportunities for us to improve ourselves, however low we sink.

In this book I concentrate on some of the very best case studies and they are presented for the reader to make his or her own judgement. This is not a scientific book, though it draws heavily on the work of a number of eminent scientists. Some of the accounts are simply based on the testimony of reputable

and trustworthy individuals. Though there are still many questions that remain unanswered about reincarnation and much
more research to be done before science as a whole begins to
accept the evidence, I believe there is already a great deal of
impressive evidence available.

What is beyond dispute is that acceptance of reincarnation
dominates the beliefs and actions of a very large number of
people. I hope that, after reading this book, you will view this
life, and your possible future lives, from a new perspective.

Roy Stemman
October 1996

chapter one

FAMOUS BELIEVERS

MILITARY BELIEVERS

An army officer was about to show a newly arrived general around the superb Roman ruins at the French town of Langres when the visitor told him: 'You don't have to. I know this place. I know it well.' He then directed the driver around the ruins, pointing out various landmarks, including the drill ground, the temples of Mars and Apollo, the forum and the amphitheatre. Yet he was an American and it was the first time he had visited the town in which he was about to assume his first command – at least in this life. His arrival at Langres, it seems, had stirred a memory of a life he had once lived as one of Caesar's legionaries.

What makes this story particularly interesting is the identity of the person involved. The general was not an unknown military man but the remarkable American hero of the Second World War, General George 'Blood and Guts' Patton, victor of the Battle of the Bulge. And this was just one of a number of past lives he recalled in which he had been a warrior, suggesting that we develop skills and carry them with us from one life to the next.

General Patton could also remember, for example, being at the walls of Tyre with Alexander the Great. He was equally certain that he had been a member of the Greek phalanx which met Cyrus II, the Persian conqueror who founded the Achaemenid empire more than 500 years before the birth of Christ. Long before his successes in the Second World War, Patton could recall fighting in the Hundred Years' War on Crécy's field. And he also remembered serving as a general

1

with Joachim Murat, the brilliant eighteenth-century cavalry leader who was one of Napoleon's most famous marshals and, as king of Naples, championed Italian nationalism.

As well as speaking openly about all this, the American hero captured the feelings evoked by these past-life memories in a poem, 'Through a Glass Darkly', which he wrote in 1944. One of the verses said:

> So as through a glass and darkly
> The age-long strife I see
> Where I fought in many guises
> Many names – but always me!

General Patton died in Germany the following year, after an automobile accident at Mannheim.

A little over a month before General Patton's death, another Second World War hero – Lord Dowding – was causing a sensation in England with his outspoken views on life after death. Dowding, who directed the Battle of Britain as Air Chief Marshal of the Royal Air Force, should have attended Oxford University at the end of October, in the company of General Dwight D. Eisenhower and Field Marshal Montgomery, to receive the honorary award of Doctor of Civil Laws. Instead, he preferred to honour a speaking engagement which clashed with the presentation and so he spoke at the Theosophical Society's meeting at Kingsway Hall, London.

'I have some reason to suppose,' he told his audience, 'that those who sowed the seeds of abominable cruelty at the time of the Inquisition reaped their own harvest at Belsen and Buchenwald.'

It was, to say the least, a controversial view, since it portrayed the victims of the Holocaust as individuals who were simply being punished in the death camps for their misdeeds in previous lives. Many people were angered by his claim, and were quick to point out the pitfalls of such thinking. Who are the victims and who the perpetrators? Like the chicken and the egg, it is impossible to know who came first.

However, Lord Dowding was used to such controversy and was well able to cope with his critics. He had first revealed his interest in Spiritualism in his 1943 book *Many Mansions*, and his views on reincarnation appeared in a sequel two years later called *Lychgate: The Entrance to the Path*. In these books he described how he had received spirit messages from dead soldiers, sailors and airmen, all victims of the war, through a non-professional medium in south-west London.

It seems that his belief in reincarnation was not only based on mediumistic messages but also on his own experiences. For he told his London audience that, whilst it was given to some human beings to revisit the scenes of their past lives, others – like himself – were given glimpses through the eyes of seers or the Akashic records (which he described as a permanent record of all humanity's thoughts and actions: a more complex version, perhaps, of Jung's collective consciousness) and that such glimpses were not for self-glorification.

'I am by nature the most insular and intolerant Englishman,' he explained:

> I am like the man who, after the last war, said the League of Nations would be a very good idea if it was not for all those damned foreigners! But if you happen to be a person like that, and you learn from evidence which you are prepared to accept that in the past you have been a Chinese, an Egyptian, a Persian, a Red Indian, whatever it may have been, you begin to assume a somewhat less exclusive view of these our fellow men.

General Patton and Air Chief Marshal Lord Dowding are by no means the only fighting men to have believed in reincarnation. Others include Napoleon Bonaparte (1767–1815), general and Emperor of the French, and one of the most celebrated figures in history. He was certain he had lived as the Emperor Charlemagne, king of the Franks, 10,000 years earlier. And Emperor Julian the Apostate (331–363), the last Roman emperor to attempt to replace Christianity with paganism, believed he was the reincarnation of Alexander the Great (356–323 BC), king of Macedonia and one of the world's greatest generals.

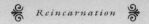

SHOWBUSINESS BELIEVERS

Belief in reincarnation is, of course, widespread and those who have declared their interest in the subject are to be found in virtually every discipline. Asked to name a famous person who believes in reincarnation, most people would put actress Shirley MacLaine top of the list. She, more than any other celebrity in recent times, has been an outspoken champion of past lives through her accounts of life as a maidservant in ancient Egypt, as a model for Toulouse Lautrec in France, or as an Atlantean. She may strike many as gullible in the extreme, but she is not alone in her profession. A list of famous believers in reincarnation sometimes reads like a *Hollywood Who's Who*.

Sylvester Stallone, for example, is convinced that he lived during the French Revolution, suffering a brutal and bloody death which even his film character Rambo would have found difficult to avoid: he was decapitated by the guillotine. John Travolta, who shot to stardom in *Saturday Night Fever*, suspects that he was also a film actor in his past life – perhaps even Rudolf Valentino. Singer Engelbert Humperdinck is just as certain he has lived ninety-five previous lives, including one as a Roman emperor. I am not sure who actor Martin Sheen was in his previous existence but he is a firm believer in reincarnation, arguing that families do not come together by chance. 'Our children,' he explains, 'come to us to make up for indiscretions in past lives. They are hold-overs from lifetimes we have not solved.' Singer Stevie Nicks is adamant that this is her last life on Earth, having lived before as an Egyptian high priestess, a concert pianist and a victim of the Holocaust. Under hypnosis, composer Henry Mancini is said to have discovered that he is the reincarnation of nineteenth-century Italian composer Giuseppe Verdi, whose works include *Rigoletto*, *La Traviata*, *Aida*, *Otello* and *Falstaff*, and before that he had been an engineer for the building of the Great Pyramid at Giza, and an officer in the court of Montezuma, the last Aztec emperor in Mexico.

Tina Turner has even searched for evidence of a past life in

Egypt, having been told by a Californian psychic that she is the reincarnation of Hatshepsut, a woman who ruled that country as pharaoh for almost twenty years. This clearly struck a chord with her.

As for Loretta Swit, best known for her role as Major 'Hot Lips' Houlihan in the long-running TV series *M*A*S*H*, glimpses of a past life have persuaded her that she was once a powerful, eleventh-century Chinese landowner who ruled over a large estate and whose word was law. That life seems to impinge on this one: 'I have Chinese rugs, statues, vases and I used to have Pekinese dogs. I just feel so comfortable surrounding myself with such things. Even my housekeeper is Chinese.'

The late Kenny Everett, a zany and flamboyant English radio disc jockey and television personality, is also on record as having been a believer in reincarnation. Appearing on a TV chat show, he told the host that his wife, Lee, a medium, had told him that in a previous life he had been her son and before that he had been a Spanish nun. Later, in an interview before he died of Aids, Everett said with typical humour: 'I can't imagine I was nowhere before this. I'd like to come back living in Italy or Spain or somewhere. As long as I don't come back bald or living in Bosnia, I don't mind.'

His wife of twelve years, Lee Everett, has now written a book, *Celebrity Regressions*, in which she tells of the past-life memories of a number of celebrities who allowed her to regress them. She is well qualified to do so: as well as being a medium and psychic during her marriage to Everett she also conducted past-life therapy, in which she now specialises. Among those featured in the book is Elton John, who recalled three lives including one as an eighteenth-century composer who lived in France and died in Venice. Comedian Jimmy Tarbuck remembered a life in which he was a knight who died after being struck by an arrow while fighting alongside his king. Ballet dancer Wayne Sleep remembered being stabbed to death in a warehouse on the Thames. And actress Fenella Fielding was certain that the life she saw under hypnosis, in which she was a man, had been lived in Peru – even though she has never been there.

These colourful, headline-grabbing accounts may delight the stars' PR representatives and be very meaningful to the celebrities concerned, but their anecdotal nature adds little to our knowledge or understanding of this complex subject, apart from illustrating how widespread is the belief in reincarnation, or perhaps how fertile our imaginations can be.

Occasionally, however, a remark is made by a celebrity which demonstrates that his or her views are deeply held and the result of much soul-searching. Judith Durham, one-time singer with talented sixties pop group The Seekers, and now enjoying a comeback as a solo artist, is a firm believer in reincarnation. Her husband Ron Edgeworth died in 1995 after years of suffering from the wasting Motor Neurone Disease. 'My wish is that Ron has had his last birth and is now with God,' she said in an interview shortly after his death. 'But he could already be in a womb somewhere. We said our farewells and I have no wish to see him again, even though I am still attached to him in my heart.'

WHAT DOES BELIEVING IN REINCARNATION REALLY MEAN?

Such celebrities can speak openly of their New Age beliefs, confident that talking of past lives will not damage their careers any more than a confession that they consult astrologers and tarot card readers or place crystals in strategic places around their homes or on their bodies to enhance their powers. Today, almost anything goes. But at least, in the West, and increasingly so in the rest of the world, we are encouraged to think for ourselves (a right that was denied to millions of people, over many centuries, who were told by either the state or the Church what they could and could not believe).

It is important to appreciate, also, that there is no universal agreement among those who believe in reincarnation. In fact, there are often fundamental disagreements on the mechanics, frequency, selectiveness and purpose of rebirth. The only common belief is that the soul will return in another body and that is a view shared by over half the world's population.

Around the globe, the burial grounds of past civilisations

testify to the fact that early man believed in an after-life. Everyday items were buried with the dead for use in the next life. In time, ideas about the after-life changed and – perhaps based on memories – the concept of reincarnation was introduced. The Egyptians believed, some 4,000 years ago, that their pharaohs would reincarnate and, in time, extended this possibility to others. Reincarnation is also referred to in India's earliest known writings – composed around 3,500 years ago – and is an integral part of two of its major religions, Hinduism and Buddhism. The Hindus were the first to incorporate the belief, some 5,000 years ago, and it remains a vital concept for the 500 million who follow its teachings today. Many of its ideas are to be found in Buddhism, which is only half as old and currently has some 200 million followers. Like Hinduism, there are many versions of Buddhism today, the principal one being Tibetan, led by the Dalai Lama, in which rebirth and karma play important roles. Ancient Chinese Taoists also accepted reincarnation.

Hinduism gave birth to Sikhism and Jainism in India, which both accept reincarnation. So, too, does the mystical Islamic sect known as the Sufis; the Druse religion of Syria; and certain Jewish sects who follow the mystical teachings contained in the Kabbala.

As for Christianity, there is no doubt that some of its early followers were firm believers in rebirth, but few people today find any support for this in biblical teachings (though some texts *can* be interpreted as having a reincarnation slant). The reason for its absence, argue the believers, is that Emperor Justinian condemned the belief at a local synod in AD 543 and outlawed it, along with other teachings, ten years later at the Second Council of Constantinople. The Emperor did this by declaring his 'Anathemas against Origen'. Origen, who lived from AD 185–254 and was described by St Jerome as 'the greatest teacher of the Church after the apostles', took the view that:

> Every soul ... comes into this world strengthened by the victories or weakened by the defeats of its previous life.

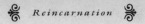

Its place in this world, as a vessel appointed to honour or dishonour, is determined by its previous merits or demerits. Its work in this world determines its place in the world which is to follow this ...

Having been tortured and imprisoned for his views, Origen's reputation suffered further after his death when Emperor Justinian's 'Anathemas' made it a sin to believe in 'the fabulous pre-existence of souls', forcing all Christians to accept that each soul was newly created to enter the body of a newborn baby.

WHY DO PEOPLE BELIEVE IN REINCARNATION?

Religious convictions and attitudes shape the thinking of many – though past-life memories sometimes provide the basis for belief in reincarnation. However, many prominent individuals who have declared their acceptance of rebirth have not recorded their reasons.

Was it, then, some personal experience which led the great automobile entrepreneur, Henry Ford, to declare: 'I believe that we are here now and will come back ... Of this I am sure ... that we are here for a purpose. And that we go on. Mind and memory – they are the eternals'? He later amplified this view, when he said: 'Genius is experience. Some seem to think that it is a gift or talent, but it is the fruit of long experience in many lives. Some are older souls than others, and so they know more.'

Composer Richard Wagner (1813–1883), whose best-known works include *The Flying Dutchman*, *Tannhäuser* and *The Ring of the Nibelungs*, seems to have owed his unshakable belief in reincarnation to logic. After a deep study of the subject he declared that 'in contrast to reincarnation and karma all other views appear petty and narrow,' adding, 'I cannot take my life, for the Will to accomplish the Object of Art would draw me back into life again until I realised that Object, and so I would only be re-entering this circle of tears and misery.'

Perhaps it was also the 'logic' of reincarnation which led Bohemian-born Gustav Mahler (1860–1911), noted for his symphonies and songs, to tell his close friend and biographer Richard Specht in 1895:

We all return; it is this certainty that gives meaning to life and it does not make the slightest difference whether or not in a later incarnation we remember the former life. What counts is not the individual and his comfort, but the great aspiration to the perfect and the pure which goes on in each incarnation.

Some politicians have openly expressed their belief in reincarnation – hardly a vote-winning issue – among them the great Liberal, David Lloyd George (1863–1945), British prime minister from 1916 to 1922. The man who laid the foundation for the modern welfare state said: 'The conventional Heaven, with its angels perpetually singing, etc., nearly drove me mad in my youth and made me an atheist for ten years. My opinion is that we shall be reincarnated.'

And Count Leo Tolstoy (1828–1910), author of some of the world's greatest novels, including *War and Peace* and *Anna Karenina*, expressed a view of eternal life which was unusual for his time, but very much in line with some schools of thought today: '... our life is but one of the dreams of the more real life, and so it is endlessly, until the very last one, a very real one – the life of God.'

Perhaps he was influenced by the experiences of a distant relative, the dramatist, novelist and poet Count A.K. Tolstoy (1817–1875), much of whose poetry was set to music by Tchaikovsky, Mussorgsky, Rimsky-Korsakov and others. He was apparently certain that he had lived in Asia in a former life.

Similarly, Christmas Humphries, founder of the Buddhist Society in England, did not base his belief in reincarnation entirely on the teachings of Buddhism. He was convinced he had been sentenced to death some 3,300 years ago during the reign of Egypt's Rameses II for making love to a Virgin of Isis

– a girl priest who had sworn, in honour of the goddess, to refrain from sex.

And I particularly like the view of a scientist, Professor C.J. Ducasse (1881–1969), former chairman of the Department of Philosophy at Brown University, president of the American Philosophical Association, and second vice-president of the American Society for Psychical Research, who said in 1958:

> Whether or not survival as plurality of lives on earth [reincarnation] is a fact, it is at least coherently thinkable and not incompatible with any facts known to us today. Of all the conceptions of the significance of human life on earth, the reincarnation hypothesis, which regards each life of a person as being like a day in school, is the only one that makes any sense. How come one person is born a genius and another a boob; one is born beautiful and another ugly; one is born healthy and another crippled? The concept of rebirth on earth, perhaps after an interval occupied by the individual in distilling out of memories of a life just ended such wisdom as his reflective powers enabled him to extract, would enable us to believe there is justice in the universe.

Finally, the English philosopher Professor C.D. Broad of Cambridge University, presenting the Thirteenth F.W.H. Myers Memorial Lecture entitled 'Personal Identity and Survival', declared: 'Speaking for myself, I would say that [reincarnation] seems to me on general grounds to be much the most plausible form of the doctrine of survival …' This was a view he had held for many years, as a quote from one of his scholarly books, written in 1938, shows. Here he told the reader that the theory of pre-existence and plurality of lives seemed to him to be one 'which ought to be taken very seriously, both on philosophical grounds and as furnishing a reasonable motive for right action …'

What all the individuals quoted above have in common, apart from their eminence in their chosen fields, is a belief that when this life comes to an end the soul continues its journey into another dimension and then, almost certainly, returns to earth in a different body to have new experiences and learn new lessons. The majority of them have a deep conviction inspired either by their own past-life memories or by an inner 'knowledge'.

But is the evidence for reincarnation really strong enough to convince those of us who have no conscious past-life memories? And do those who believe in rebirth take full account of the alternative explanations, ranging from wishful thinking to false memory syndrome?

Read the many case histories that follow, and judge for yourself.

chapter two

UNFINISHED BUSINESS

'THIS IS NOT MY HOME'

Within a few years of the birth of their son Mounzer in 1960, Lebanese bus driver Kamal Salim Haïdar and his wife Edma had a problem on their hands. The boy insisted on being called Jamil. Understandably, they preferred to use the name they had given him, even though there were times when he would refuse to respond to it. Eventually the three-year-old dropped that demand but replaced it with another.

'This is not my home,' Mounzer told them. 'I am from the other side.'

As he said this, he pointed in the direction of the mountains beyond Choueifate and asked to be taken to his real home. He made this request repeatedly and even stopped eating for three days because his parents refused.

By now, Mounzer was giving a wealth of detail about the person he claimed to be – Jamil Souki who lived in Aley. He revealed that he had died in battle and gave graphic descriptions of events surrounding his short life and sudden death from a bullet in the abdomen. He even told his mother that when he dreamed it was not of her but of his 'Souki' mother.

The Haïdars were Druses – members of a religion which accepts reincarnation – but they were certain their young son's memories were confused. Though they had no direct association with them, Kamal and Edma Haïdar knew of the Soukis and believed they all lived in the same town as they did: Choueifate, about 6 miles (10 kilometres) from Beirut city centre, just east of the Beirut International Airport and in the foothills of the mountains.

For that reason they made no attempt to verify Mounzer's claims.

Their attitude to his past-life memories changed, however, when Mounzer visited an aunt in Beirut who mentioned his claims to another tenant in her apartment block. This woman was a cousin of Jamil Souki and she immediately fetched a photograph which she placed before him.

'Who are they?' she asked.

'It is my mother and me,' Mounzer replied.

The photograph was of Jamil Souki and his mother Wadad.

As a result of this, Mounzer began making visits to the Soukis in Aley, a town between Beirut and Damascus, 9 miles (15 kilometres) from his home town. The Soukis also visited him in Choueifate. During these reunions he identified various people and described events about which he, as Mounzer, could not have known.

Jamil Souki had taken an interest in politics in his youth and joined the Parti Populaire Syrien (PPS) which was working for a union between Lebanon and Syria. When civil war broke out in the summer of 1958, Jamil supported President Chamoun. The intervention of the United States Marines ended the fighting but not soon enough to save the life of Jamil Souki. He was killed in battle on 4 July 1958.

Mounzer Haïdar correctly recognised Jamil's mother, younger brother and sisters. He told the family they had moved since his death, identified the house in which they had lived when he was alive and recognised the closet where Jamil Souki's clothes were kept. In one of Jamil's jackets he found three pens and insisted that one was missing. This was correct; Jamil's sister Ibtysame had taken it with her to Venezuela. He also identified which of three keys he found in a wallet was the one to Jamil's valise. Speaking as if he were Jamil, Mounzer recalled his brother Najeeb's emigration to the USA, when he had gone to the quay to say 'goodbye'. He also told Jamil's mother he had written her a letter a few days before he died and asked whether she had received it. She had. Mounzer recalled that when Jamil died he had 31 Lebanese pounds in his pocket. Wadad Souki confirmed that this was the exact amount she had taken from the pocket of her dead son when his clothes were returned. Mounzer even knew that Jamil had once tied his brother Ghassan to a bed for a couple of hours because he had misbehaved.

Sometimes Mounzer identified a person by name. At other times he correctly stated their relationship to Jamil. There were tests to see how accurate he was in recognising people but occasionally this happened quite spontaneously. For example, spotting Jamil's cousin in the street, four-year-old Mounzer ran to Jamil's aunt and said: 'Look! There is Abdullah Abu El Abed.' Two years later a similar incident occurred while he was visiting Aley. Mounzer left the group he was with and went up to a complete stranger, saying: 'You are Ramez.' The man he had recognised was Ramez Kassis, Jamil's best friend. Another of Jamil's friends, Jamil Rishdan Sawaya, who had been with him at the Battle of Chamlane, heard of Mounzer's claim and decided to check for himself. Together with a companion, he went to the Haïdars' home in Choueifate, where the two men gave false names and claimed to be journalists (the story had already appeared in newspapers and one magazine even pictured young Mounzer on the battlefield re-enacting Jamil's actions). They were invited in and Mounzer was called to speak to them. As soon as the five-year-old saw them he said, 'Oh, Jamil Sawaya', embraced him and sat next to him. On yet another occasion, when young Mounzer was attending a funeral, he went up to Arif Souki and said 'You are my Uncle Arif.'

'How is that?' asked the man.

'I am Jamil Souki, your nephew. I was killed at Chamlane.'

Though he was not able to identify Jamil's girlfriend Iffat Zahr by name, his behaviour showed his feelings towards her. Mounzer was nine years old when he first met her and he sat beside her during the entire visit to her house. He refused to eat when other people offered him food but only ate when she took him to the dining room. When he had finished eating, Iffat asked him to give the special salute of the Parti Populaire

Syrien and Mounzer gave the salute exactly. He also correctly stated that he – as Jamil – had given her a photograph of the PPS leader, Antoun Saadeh, and the group's emblem. Only her immediate family knew of these gifts.

This remarkable case in just one of thousands which have been researched by Canadian-born Professor Ian Stevenson, the world's foremost expert on the scientific investigation of reincarnation. Mounzer Haïdar's story is presented in great depth in the third volume of Stevenson's *Cases Suggestive of Reincarnation*. Using local interpreters, Professor Stevenson began investigating the case in March 1968, three or four years after the two families had met. He interviewed both the Haïdars and the Soukis as well as various other witnesses.

Quite apart from the detail which Mounzer Haïdar was able to supply about the life he appeared to remember, an impressive aspect of this case – and not unusual in reincarnation reports – was the strong urge the young child had to see his former family. It was as if, having been cut off in his prime on the battlefield, he had an overwhelming need to return to that former life and continue from where he had left it.

'Mounzer made a number of visits to the Souki family in Aley and was continuing to do so up to March 1972, the time of my last visit to Aley,' Professor Stevenson writes. 'He had passed five days with the Soukis a month before. He enjoyed his visits to the Souki family ... immensely.'

Sadly for Mounzer, these came to an end when the Soukis decided to emigrate to Venezuela – where one of their daughters had already gone to live. Before leaving, Wadad Souki gave Jamil's clothes to Mounzer and continued to write to him from her new home in South America. By this time his vivid memories of the life he had lived as Jamil Souki had faded – which is typical of such cases – but his affection for his former family clearly remained.

THE BOY WHO LOST HIS FAMILY

Not surprisingly, announcements by young children, soon after they learn to speak, that they are someone else and want to be taken to where they belong are not usually welcomed by their families. Various measures are often taken to rid them of their memories or silence them.

So, when Prakash Varshnay, aged four-and-a-half, declared that he was really called Nirmal and began running out into the street with the intention of going home to his father Bholanath in Kosi Kalan – a town in the District of Mathura, Uttar Pradesh, India – his parents were deeply upset. This happened four or five nights in a row until his uncle promised to take him by bus to Kosi Kalan. Instead, he took a bus going in the opposite direction but Prakash immediately told him they were on the wrong bus. They got the right bus and eventually went to the shop owned by Bholanath Jain, whose son Nirmal had died at the age of ten in April 1950, sixteen months before Prakash was born. But the shop was closed, Prakash failed to recognise it and they returned home to Chhatta without meeting anyone, though members of the Jain family did learn of his visit later.

Despite the apparent failure of the mission, Prakash, who was born in August 1951 and was now five years old, continued to insist that he was Nirmal and demanded his return to Kosi Kalan. He also complained about the mediocrity of the house in which they lived, spoke of his 'father's' shops and named relatives. Often he would weep for long periods and go without food while pleading to go to Kosi Kalan. Among the actions taken by his parents to stamp out these memories was to turn him anti-clockwise on a potter's wheel, which is traditionally supposed to impair past-life memory. It did not work, so they beat him.

Prakash was ten years old when Jagdish Jain, one of Bholanath's younger sons, learned of the boy's claim after moving back to Kosi Kalan from Delhi. Shortly afterwards, his father Bholanath went to Chhatta on business, taking his daughter Memo with him, and decided to meet the youngster who claimed to be the reincarnation of his dead son. Prakash recognised him and called him 'father'. He also said the daughter who was with him was Vimla. This was wrong, but interestingly Memo had not been born when Nirmal Jain died. He did, however, have a sister named Vimla who was then about Memo's age. When the father and daughter left Chhatta, Prakash went with them to the bus station and pleaded unsuccessfully for them to take him back with them. A few days later, Nirmal's mother, older sister Tara and brother Devendra, impressed with what they had heard, went to visit Prakash, who wept with joy when he saw Tara and begged his father to let him return to Kosi Kalan. Again, this was refused.

Eventually the Jain family persuaded Prakash's parents to let him visit their town and when he arrived he led the way from the bus station to their house. There, he recognised Nirmal's other brother and various relatives and neighbours, as well as identifying the room in which Nirmal had slept and also the one he had been moved to before he died of chickenpox.

By now, feelings were running high between the two families and some Varshnay members were convinced that the Jains were going to try to adopt Prakash permanently. This animosity reached its peak when the Varshnays put a stop to the visits but it gradually diminished and eventually the two families exchanged gifts and the Varshnays again permitted the child to visit the Jains.

Even though Prakash's family thought he had stopped visiting the Jains when he reached his teenage years, it has since come to light that he still felt he had 'unfinished business' with his former family in 1964. He was then visiting Kosi Kalan once or twice a month even though Nirmal's parents had both died. He went mainly to see Jagdish Jain, Nirmal's older brother, with whom he clearly enjoyed a very happy relationship.

Critics often ask why such cases are always from the Far East or Middle East. The answer – as this book demonstrates – is that they are not. It is true, however, that the cultures of some countries predispose families towards accepting the claims of children who say they can remember a past life. On the other hand, as with the Varshnays, belief in reincarnation does not automatically mean that a child's statements will be encouraged.

JENNY COCKELL - MOTHER OF *YESTERDAY'S CHILDREN*

One of the most remarkable recent cases of 'unfinished business' comes from England. Jenny Cockell could remember details of a former life in Ireland, as a woman named Mary, from her earliest childhood. But, whereas such memories usually fade with the passage of time, in her case they remained as vivid as ever and she consulted a hypnotist in the hope of completing the jigsaw.

She was a Northamptonshire housewife with two children when, largely through her own detective work, she identified the Irish town of Malahide as the place where she had lived. She also knew that she had given birth to eight children in that life and that she had died in hospital soon after the birth of the last one, a daughter.

Jenny Cockell told the story in her international bestseller which was published in the UK as *Yesterday's Children* just a few weeks before I launched *Reincarnation International Magazine*. It was perfect timing, for it enabled me to carry an interview with her as well as a review of her book in our first issue – and demonstrate that convincing reincarnation cases were not confined to the Far East. Since then, I have met Jenny and Sonny, her eldest son from that previous life, on a number of occasions – mostly TV studios where we have been invited to talk about the subject of rebirth – and they never fail to impress me with their straightforward, take-it-or-leave-it approach to their remarkable story.

One of the most impressive aspects of this case did not occur until after the book appeared in print. By then, Jenny had revealed that the woman whose life she was remembering was Mary Sutton, who had indeed had eight children. What had happened, after her death, was that her husband – a violent alcoholic – had been unable to care for the children and all but one of them, the eldest boy, Sonny, had been sent to foster homes. The boys had eventually found each other after many years, and had a reunion, but it was not until her book was written and in the process of being published, that all the surviving members of Mary Sutton's family came together for the first time to meet each other ... and Jenny Cockell, the woman whose past-life memories had been instrumental in bringing about the reunion. Incredibly, two of Mary Sutton's children discovered they had been living just a few miles from each other without realising they were related.

Sonny, the first-born, has been the most outspoken supporter of Jenny Cockell's claims and I asked him during one of our meetings how much Jenny Cockell resembles his mother. (There *are* some similarities in appearance but they are by no means lookalikes.) Sonny's immediate response was: 'I can see my mother in her eyes.' What had clinched it for him, when he first met Jenny, was that she was able to tell him about a number of incidents when he was young, which no one else could have known anything about. For example, she spoke of the day when the children had called her because they had found an animal trapped in a snare. And she could remember standing by a jetty waiting for a boat, though she no longer remembered why. Sonny knew the answer. She was waiting for him. He used to be ferried to an island to act as caddy on its golf course. Whenever he did this, his mother would always be waiting for him on the jetty as the boat came home.

Now that she has succeeded in bringing her past-life family together again, Jenny has largely lost the feeling of 'unfinished business' that had haunted her from childhood. Her mission has been accomplished but her lively mind and natural curiosity have drawn her to continue delving into the subject of reincarnation – her own and other people's – and its implications.

THE LITTLE MONK

Before he could even talk, Duminda Bandara Ratnayake's behaviour had already started to puzzle his parents. He would place a piece of cloth over his shoulder and carry it around in the same way as monks in Sri Lanka carry their robes. This proved to be no passing phase for, as soon as he learned to speak, the only 'toys' Duminda wanted to play with were a robe and a fan. The son of Sinhalese Buddhist parents who run a small poultry farm, it may at first have been thought that the child was simply mimicking a monk he had seen. But, as soon as he could speak, Duminda began supplying information which showed these traits to be far more deep-rooted.

At the age of three, in 1987, Duminda told his parents that before his birth he had been an abbot at the Asgiriya temple and monastery in Kandy, which is one of Sri Lanka's largest and most ancient religious centres. Its monks, and those of the Malwatta temple, have the privilege of guarding the Temple of the Tooth in Kandy, which is one of Theravada Buddhism's foremost places of pilgrimage.

Duminda explained to them that he had taught other monks at Asgiriya where he had suffered a sudden pain in his chest and fallen to the floor. He had been taken to hospital by the monks, where he had died. In recounting his final moments in that past life, Duminda correctly used the word *apawathwuna*, which specifically related to the death of a monk. From that moment on, he insisted that his parents called him not by the name they had given him but by 'Podi Sadhu' which means 'Little Monk'.

Also, Duminda started to behave like a monk. He visited a Buddhist chapel close to his home every morning and night, picking flowers to take there and laying them down in a typical Buddhist fashion on his arrival. He observed great cleanliness, did not play with other children, and exuded an air of quiet calm. Duminda even recited holy scriptures. Not only did he somehow know these religious sentences or verses, which had not been taught to him at home, but he recited them as the monks do *and* in the ancient Sinhalese Buddhist language of Pali which the monks still learn.

By now, he was also telling his mother that he wanted to become a monk but she refused to allow him to wear robes, except on a few occasions. Eventually she sought the help of Ven. Iriyagama Jinasara, a monk at a nearby temple, and he saw her and the child in mid-1987 when Duminda was a little over three years old. Perhaps because of his young age, Duminda did not reply to the monk's questions. But when asked what he would like, he asked for a fan. This plays an important part in a monk's rituals and, as soon as he received it, Duminda held it in front of his face in the typical fashion and recited a Buddhist stanza. This, in the opinion of Iriyagama Jinasara, was also something he could not have learned at home.

Based on what he had seen, the monk advised the boy's mother to take him to Asgiriya monastery, which she did, accompanied by Duminda's grandparents. A journalist, Oliver D. Silva from the *Island* newspaper, who had heard about the case, was also a witness to this visit. However, it appears to have furnished little in the way of new information and provoked no new memories.

Indeed, the most surprising statements Duminda made about his previous life were unrelated to religious matters. They were highly unusual but proved to be correct. He said that he had owned a red car and an elephant, and had also missed his money bag and radio.

At no time did Duminda give the name of the person he had been in his previous life, which led the journalist to conduct his own research and conclude that he was referring to the Ven. Rathanapala, a senior monk who had died of a heart attack in 1975, in a town outside Asgiriya. But Professor Erlendur Haraldsson, a leading parapsychologist and expert on reincarnation research, based at the Department of Psychology, University of Iceland, Reykjavik, Iceland, did not agree. He first visited Sri Lanka and interviewed the boy and his family in September 1988, when Duminda was four years old, before going on to the Asgiriya temple to discuss the case with the monks. He returned to Sri Lanka again in 1989 and 1990 to complete his study, by which time Duminda's memories were beginning to fade and his behaviour had modified.

Reporting on his research in the *Journal of Scientific Exploration* (**Vol. 5**, No. 2, 1991), Professor Haraldsson explained why he thought the journalist's identification of the previous-life monk as Ven. Rathanapala was wrong:

We learned from three monks who had known him that Ven. Rathanapala had not owned a car or an elephant, had no personal income (hence no money bag), did not preach (hence did not use the fan), had no connections with the Malwatta temple, and had been known for his interest in politics. Thus, Rathanapala was excluded as a candidate for Duminda's statements.

Professor Haraldsson went on to discuss a number of other possible candidates, but only one of them was known to have owned a red car: Gunnepana Saranankara, who had been at Asgiriya for eight years before he died in 1929. He did not own a radio but was the only abbot at the monastery ever to own a gramophone. He did not, however, die in hospital, as Duminda had said, but in the Asgiriya temple. Later, the professor and his interpreter showed Duminda a very old group photograph taken at the monastery and asked him if he recognised anyone. He pointed to one figure and said, 'This was me.' At this point, they did not know the identity of anyone in the picture but later received confirmation from two old monks who knew the group well that the person Duminda had identified was, indeed, Gunnepana Saranankara.

There is, of course, an extraordinarily long interval between the monk's death in 1929 and his birth as Duminda in 1984. And it is possible that he had experienced another incarnation in between. What is certain, however, is that he seems to have returned with a very strong feeling of having 'unfinished business'. It is as if the heart attack which cut him off in his prime prevented him from teaching and preaching as much as he had intended and now, in this new life, he is determined to pick up where he left off.

'When we met the family again in November 1990,' Professor Haraldsson reports, 'his mother had yielded to his wish and he was going to enter the monastery in a year's time, which was the earliest possible age.'

These cases remind us that, however scientific we need to be in collecting and analysing data, we are still talking about real people who often feel frustrated or angry at having departed from their previous life sooner than they expected, and are eager to do something about it. For such people, the most dominant emotion in their dying moments in that previous life may have been anger that their hopes would not be fulfilled; guilt that they were leaving behind people who depended upon them; or desire to return in circumstances that would be different. This could explain why such individuals have vivid memories of their past lives, whereas the majority of us are blissfully and thankfully unaware of the dramas, disappointments, happiness and achievements that were ours in our previous incarnations.

chapter three

REUNIONS

HIS FATHER'S SON

*I*f the story of Aiz Nouhad Abu Rokon were offered to Hollywood it would probably be rejected on the grounds that it is beyond belief. Yet Aiz's remarkable and well-documented experience shows that the facts of reincarnation are often stranger than fiction, and can cause enormous complications in family relationships.

I first learned of this case in 1995 from my good friend Rona Hart, who works for the Jewish Board of Deputies in London. Rona is one of a large number of people who act as correspondents for my magazine: monitoring media coverage of reincarnation and reporting the best instances. She had just read a very well-researched *Jerusalem Post* feature by Sue Fishkoff which included several detailed reports of rebirth among the Druse, of which the case of Aiz Nouhad Abu Rokon was just one.

I contacted the newspaper immediately and was delighted when they gave us permission to reproduce the feature in full in our columns. Photographer Roni Sofer, whose pictures of the subjects illustrated the account, was similarly obliging. All the cases merit inclusion in this book, but I will confine myself to that of Aiz.

From an early age, the young boy had spoken of his previous life. At three-and-a-half, for example, he was able to tell his parents that his name had been Ali Badawi, a truck driver from Hatzbiya in southern Lebanon. Since they were Druses, their young son's statements were accepted without question but nothing was done to check his story. However, events were soon to conspire to bring Aiz's present and past-life

families together. In 1982, when he was six years old, Aiz saw
a middle-aged woman in the streets of Usfiya where he lived.
He walked straight up to her and declared, 'You're Nebiya, my
wife.' The child then told the astonished woman of her
husband's death on a snowbound country road near Baalbek,
in February 1975. He could clearly recall, as Ali Badawi,
driving alone when he was stopped by a couple of thugs
demanding money and his vehicle. Ali refused their demands
and they shot him in the shoulder and stomach, then buried
him by the side of the road.

Needless to say, Nebiya Badawi – who was visiting Usfiya to
see relatives when Aiz recognised her – was surprised and
impressed by the child's statements and kept in touch with him
and his family on her return to Lebanon. Seven more years
were to elapse before they met again. At Nebiya's invitation in
1982, the thirteen-year-old Aiz went to Lebanon to visit his
home in a previous life. His voice shakes with emotion and
tears well up in his eyes as he recalls the occasion:

> I stood on the front steps and called out to my daughter
> Leena, who was five when I died. I walked into the house
> and I knew it all so well. I went to the closet and looked
> for my clothes, all my little treasures. Everything was as I
> remembered, and the family was incredibly moved to see
> me again.

Nebiya and her family accepted Aiz as the reincarnation of Ali
and he began visiting them regularly. In fact, three years later,
when his 'daughter' from his previous life got married, it was
Aiz – then sixteen years old – who stood in as her father during
the ceremony. An understandable choice, of course, because
that's exactly how they regarded him.

In 1995 Aiz himself got married to a young Druse woman
from Ali Badawi's village and took her back to Usfiya to live.
There, on the walls of their home, they proudly display old
black-and-white photographs of Ali before his death more
than twenty years ago, alongside recent colour pictures of the
teenage Aiz with Ali's children – Nassim, Leena and Wassim,

who in 1995 were aged thirty, twenty-eight and twenty-seven respectively. Just added to the collection is a photo of a two-year-old girl, nineteen-year-old Aiz's first 'grandchild'.

The story does not end there.

A year after Aiz had made his first visit to the Badawi family in Lebanon, his father died. Nahoud Abu Rokon, a soldier in the IDF border police, was tragically killed on 1 November 1983. Three years later, a small boy named Abid Abuassi walked into the Rokons' home in Usfiya, pointed to a picture of Nahoud taken shortly before his death, and said to Aiz: 'I am your father.'

Adib's mother, Nabilla Abuassi, had realised he could remember a past life from the moment he could speak. He would constantly ask for someone named Aiz.

'I thought he meant a boy in our village of Shfaram, but when we brought him to the house, Adib said he wasn't the right Aiz. He said, "Aunt Efat knows my Aiz".'

Nabilla spoke to her sister Efat, a teacher in Usfiya, who said she had a young boy named Aiz in her class. So Nabilla decided to call the Abu Rokon home to make enquiries. As soon as she got through, young Adib almost tore the phone from her hand and shouted into the receiver that he wanted to talk to Aiz right away. As a result of his first contact, it was agreed that the Abuassis should visit the Abu Rokon home.

'Adib was so excited all the way there,' his father Kamal recalls. 'He told us exactly how to get to the house.'

And when they arrived he not only walked right in and identified his clothes in the closet but also told Aiz's mother that he had one cigarette in a jacket pocket when he died. She checked the jacket and, sure enough, there was the solitary cigarette. Adib was also able to give a graphic account of how he had died in his past life:

My unit was searching a building in Tzur, Lebanon. My best friend Sayid went inside and I stayed outside to keep watch. Suddenly something exploded inside the building – a bomb of some kind. I remember lying on the ground, looking over at Sayid. There was a huge rock on his body, and he was all covered in blood. I remember shouting, 'Sayid! Sayid! Please don't die!' I don't remember anything else.

Despite his own smoking habit in his past life, the diminutive Adib now admonishes his 'son' Aiz when he lights up a cigarette. 'Don't smoke so much,' he scolds. The grown-up Aiz frowns, shrugs ... and puts it out, because the two still relate to each other like father and son. Adib and Aiz recall, for example, an occasion when they were three and twelve years old respectively and Aiz had spoken sharply to his mother (Adib's wife in his previous incarnation). The toddler's immediate response was to smack his 'son' full in the face.

Looking back, Aiz admits, 'I deserved it,' and adds, 'I felt, he's my father, he has the right.'

In her report on this case, Sue Fishkoff made the following comments on the complicated relationships that have developed as a result of the boys' reincarnation memories:

Nabilla and Kamal try to take Aiz's and Adib's relationship in their stride. They think of Aiz as just another son, not as a grandson, and while they aren't exactly sure where Aiz's mother fits into their genealogical tree, they feel she's part of the family. And they are not shy about admitting they believe the boys' stories are true. 'How do you explain a two-and-a-half-year-old child who can direct us to a house in a town where he's never been, go to a closet and pick out another man's clothes as his own, recognise "friends" by name before he meets them, look at a photo of "himself" with his wife and know the date it was taken on the Golan?' Kamal wonders. 'These are just facts. Can you explain them?'

THE LITTLE MOTHER

In most family reunion cases, it is difficult to bring scientific judgement to bear on the facts because the friends and relatives of the individuals involved are carried along on a tide of curiosity and emotion which takes no account of the need to record statements carefully as they are uttered and before confirmation has been given. In assessing their credibility, therefore, we need to be aware that some stories might have been (perhaps unwittingly) embroidered in the telling. There are plenty of cases, however, where researchers have been able to start their investigations and make proper records either before the two families have been brought together, or very soon afterwards.

A classic case of this kind involved a girl born in Old Delhi, the Indian capital, in 1926. Kumari Shanti Devi delighted her parents by speaking of her 'husband' and 'children' when she was only three. At first, they took this childish talk to be a sign that she would marry early. But when her mother asked who this husband was, Shanti Devi replied without hesitation:

> Kedarnath. He lives in Muttra. Our house is yellow stucco with large arched doors and lattice-work windows. Our yard is large and filled with marigolds and jasmine. Great bowers of scarlet bougainvilleas climb over the house. We often sit on the veranda watching our little son play on the tile floor. Our sons are still there with their father.

By now, her parents were growing concerned for their daughter and decided to seek medical advice. Dr Reddy, their family physician, assured them that it was likely that Shanti Devi was a brilliant child just trying to get attention and that he would be able to get her to admit that what she was recounting was just fantasy. She did no such thing.

In answer to the doctor's questions she revealed that she had been named Ludgi and had died during childbirth. 'It was a very difficult pregnancy from the first,' she explained. 'I had not been well and when I knew the baby was coming I wondered if I was ready for it. Each day I felt worse and worse – and when the baby came it was a breach birth. The baby lived but the delivery killed me.'

Shanti Devi was taken from the consulting room by a nurse

while her parents and the doctor discussed what they had just heard. They agreed that it was impossible for an only child to understand in such detail the mental and physical aspects of a difficult pregnancy. But the doctor could offer no medical remedy to eradicate these memories and they remained consistent over the next four years as her parents took her from one medical man to another.

It was not until 1934, when she was eight, that Shanti Devi's story began to be taken at face value. Fortunately, her great-uncle, Professor Kishen Chand, decided to check the facts very carefully. He started by sending a letter to the address in Muttra which Shanti Devi had often mentioned, asking if there was a man named Kedarnath living there who had lost a wife in 1925.

The contents of the letter startled the person who received and opened it – a man named Kedarnath whose wife Ludgi had died in the very year mentioned and who was still grieving over his loss. But, despite being a devout Hindu, he found it difficult to believe that his wife had been reborn. Instead, he suspected it was a plot to rob him of his property, so he asked a cousin named Lal, who lived in Delhi, to meet Shanti and her family. Mr Lal did so on the pretext of doing business with Mr Devi, and the family were unaware of his connection with the recipient of the letter that had been posted some weeks before.

Shanti, now aged nine, was helping her mother in the kitchen when Mr Lal arrived. She ran to open the door and her mother soon followed to find out why her daughter had let out a scream. She discovered Shanti had thrown herself into the arms of the surprised visitor and was sobbing. 'Mother,' she explained, 'this is a cousin of my husband! He lived not far from us in Muttra and then moved to Delhi. I am so happy to see him! He must come in. I want to know about my husband and sons.' Shanti's father then arrived home and the four entered the house and Mr Lal was able to confirm all the statements she had made over the years. Professor Chand was called to join them and they decided that the next step should be to invite Kedarnath and Ludgi's favourite son to Delhi to meet the Devis.

Shanti's behaviour on their arrival was revealing. She tried to scoop up her 'son', who was much bigger than her, and smothered him with kisses. She also called him by her own pet names. She then served Kedarnath with biscuits and cheese in a dutiful way so typical of Ludgi that Kedarnath's eyes filled with tears. On seeing this, she tried to console him, using endearing phrases which only he and his wife had known. But he refused to leave his son with the Devis, as they requested, and found the episode disturbing.

News of this encounter reached the ears of Desh Bandu Gupta, President of the All-India Newspaper Association and a member of the Indian parliament, who decided it was imperative that the case be fully investigated. He arranged for Shanti and her parents, accompanied by himself, an advocate named Tara C. Mathur, and a contingent of scholars, scientists, reporters and well-educated citizens, to travel to Muttra.

As their train pulled in, Shanti let out a squeal of delight and started waving to several people whom she correctly identified as her husband's mother and brother. And when she stepped off the train and spoke to them, she used not the Hindustani she had learned in Delhi but the dialect of the Muttra district. The scientific committee then piled into waiting carriages for the greatest test of all: to see whether Shanti Devi could direct them to Ludgi's home. The child issued instructions, pausing only twice when she seemed uncertain, and the procession eventually stopped when she told them to do so. 'This is the house,' she declared, 'but it is a different colour. In my day it was yellow; now it is white.'

This was absolutely correct. It was the home Ludgi had shared with Kedarnath – but from which he and his sons had moved after her death. She was then taken to Kedarnath's home and immediately identified two sons by name but did not recognise the child whose birth had cost Ludgi her life. The committee next took Shanti Devi to visit Ludgi's mother, an elderly woman who was clearly confused and terrified to be confronted by a young girl who acted and talked like her daughter and knew things which only Ludgi had known. Shanti told Desh Gupta that there used to be a well on the property and, when he dug at the spot she indicated, he found it, covered with planks and dirt. Kedarnath then asked her what Ludgi had done with several rings she had hidden shortly before her death. She told him they were buried in a pot in a garden of the old home and the investigating committee found them.

Not surprisingly, this case excited tremendous interest. Crowds gathered outside Shanti and Kedarnath's homes and the story was reported prominently around the world. All of which did nothing to help Shanti Devi come to terms with her past-life memories. It was clearly impossible for her to return to her past-life 'husband', who displayed apprehension rather than affection, nor could she care for her sons. Instead, acting on the advice of others, she learned to control her love for the family in Muttra and distance herself from them.

Nearly a quarter of a century after the events described above, in 1958, a reporter found Shanti living a quiet life in Delhi as a government employee. But she refused to give any more information about the case.

'I do not wish to revive my past lives, either this one or my previous existence in Muttra,' she explained. 'It has been very difficult for me to bury my desire to return to my family. I do not want to open that closed door again.'

This is, as we shall see in later chapters, a problem with which many others have found it difficult to come to terms, and one of the reasons why the majority of us should be grateful that we do not have these memories.

THE DAUGHTER WHO CAME BACK

A reunion between a reincarnated daughter and her mother in South Africa came about after Uvashnee Rattan, a four-year-old Indian girl living with her parents in Lotusville, just outside Verulam, was taken to the nearby suburb of New Glasgow. Jugdees Rattan had to deliver a load of sand to a house there, and he took Uvashnee, and his two other children, along for the ride. Somehow the sight of the house seemed to unlock past-life memories in the young child.

On her return home she ran to her mother, declaring:

'Mommy, Mommy, my name is Sudima and I was staying at Kemla's house. Kemla's house is in New Glasgow. It is down a steep hill. The house is bluey in colour and inside there are planks ...' She went on to say that her 'other family' ate only potato curry and roti, but no meat, and that in front of her 'other' house there had been a pond and, next to that, a river where they used to wash their clothes.

Her mother asked her why she was no longer with this other family.

'Because I got sick and died. I had a bad stomach pain and died. They thought I was dead but I wasn't. I was only sleeping.'

Uvashnee's mother decided to find out if any of what her young daughter was saying was true. She suspected that maybe she had seen someone at the house when her husband delivered the sand and that this had led her to create the story. She called at the house and spoke to Jemla's maternal grandmother who told her she did not know anyone named Sudima. But the 'other' family, when they learned of the conversation, invited Mrs Rattan and her daughter to visit them. When they arrived there were several guests and Uvashnee was asked many questions which she answered fully and without hesitation. Then something extraordinary happened. Jugdees Rattan takes up the story:

Uvashnee was sitting on my wife's lap at the time. I pointed to a tray of sweetmeats near to her and said, 'Give your mother some sweetmeats, Uvashnee.' I expected that she would simply take some, then turn around and give them to my wife, but instead she got off her lap, collected some sweetmeats from the tray and took them to an elderly lady, Mrs Baghwandeen, who was sitting on the far side of the room. This woman began to cry. She took the sweetmeats from Uvashnee, pulled her onto her lap and kissed her. She said she was crying for her daughter, Anishta, who had died of dysentery twenty years before, at the age of nine. Anishta had only been sick for a day and there had been nothing anyone could

32

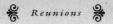

do for her. She then explained that although her daughter's name was Anishta, she also had another name bestowed on her by a priest at birth, according to Indian custom: Anishta's priest's name for her was Sudima.

This case was investigated by psychic researchers Professor David Scott-McNab and Professor John Poynton who satisfied themselves that Uvashnee's statements were genuine.

'Uvashnee has information which could not have come to her through her normal senses,' they concluded. 'It is a classical case, an extremely clear-cut case of recall of an apparent previous existence.'

And there was an unusual twist to the story which suggests that children who have such memories can sometimes also display a psychic sensitivity to members of their past-life families. In 1975 Uvashnee declared: 'You know, I feel very sorry for the other mommy. She will die very soon.' A few days later Mrs Baghwandeen died after a period of ill-health – leaving Uvashnee with the memory of their brief but happy reunion.

chapter four

FAMILY AFFAIR

Unhappy Daughter, Unhappy Son

During her short life, Emilia Lorenz was a troubled soul. Her nineteen years on earth were constantly clouded by inner conflicts which baffled her family. Freedom was what she most desired but, as a Brazilian woman, she found it hard to attain. She expressed to her brothers and sisters her dissatisfaction with being female and told them that, if there were such a thing as reincarnation, she would return next time as a man. Emilia, who was born in Brazil on 4 February 1902, also said she expected to die single and she ensured this prediction came true by rejecting a number of marriage proposals. Her one passion seems to have been sewing, at which she alone in the family excelled. Her genius with a needle was so great, in fact, that a sewing machine was bought for her.

Eventually, however, Emilia's extreme unhappiness with life culminated in several suicide attempts. She was forced to drink large amounts of milk as an antidote to the arsenic she swallowed on one occasion. But finally her life ended on 21 October 1921, very soon after she took cyanide.

Ida Lorenz, Emilia's mother, then began receiving messages from her daughter at Spiritualist meetings in which she said she regretted her suicide and wanted to be born again to her mother. 'Mamma, take me as your son. I will come as your son,' she said.

The first child born to the Lorenzes had been a son, Emilio, who had died in infancy. Emilia, named after him, was their second child. By the time her daughter committed suicide, Ida Lorenz had given birth to ten more children and was not expecting to become pregnant again. But she conceived once more and her thirteenth child, a boy whom they named Paulo, was born on 3 February 1923.

Paulo Lorenz was an unusual child. From the moment he could make his feelings known he resolutely refused to wear boys' clothes. He would either wear girls' clothes or none at all. He also like to play with girls and dolls, displayed great sewing skills, and made several remarks identifying himself with Emilia. Paulo even told some of his sisters that he was a girl. It was only when someone came up with the idea of making him a pair of trousers from a skirt which had belonged to Emilia, when he was around four or five years old, that Paulo warmed to the idea of wearing boys' clothes and slowly his masculinity began to assert itself. He recognised how the garment had been produced and commented, 'Who would have said that, after using this material in a skirt, I would later use it for trousers?'

Gradually the family began to notice other traits which suggested that Paulo was the reincarnation of his sister. The most important of these was his uncanny sewing skill. Once, for example, when he was, according to the witness, 'extremely small' he saw one of the family's servants clumsily trying to work the sewing machine. Paulo pushed her aside, showed her how it worked and proceeded to complete the demonstration by making a small sack. At the age of four he saw his sister Florzinha having trouble threading the machine and he showed her how to do it. Another sister, Marta, left some unfinished embroidery on the sewing machine and Paulo completed it for her. All this happened before he had been given any lessons on how to use it. When asked how he could do such things, Paulo responded simply: 'I knew already how to sew.' Yet, once he began to grow up, he lost his love of sewing and his sisters' skill soon overtook his.

Interestingly, Paulo also had a milk phobia – refusing to drink it all his life. This was true of Emilia too, but only in her later years and probably because she had been forced to drink large quantities of milk after the suicide attempt.

By 1962, when Paulo Lorenz was thirty-nine years old, he

was still unmarried and showed little interest in women apart from his sisters, although the intense feminine traits that were evident in his teens were no longer so apparent. In fact, he joined the Brazilian Army but retired early through ill-health with the rank of sergeant. He had pulmonary tuberculosis which required treatment and convalescence over several years.

Later Paulo became involved in local politics but after the President of Brazil, João Goulart, was deposed by a military insurrection in 1963, Paulo became increasingly concerned that he was being watched by government agents. These apparent delusions reached the point where his family decided he needed psychiatric treatment but sadly, before any action could be taken, Paulo committed suicide. He had made threats and earlier attempts but in September 1966, while staying with his sister Lola Moreira, he went into the bathroom, poured inflammable liquid over himself and set his clothes and body on fire. He died ten hours later without expressing any regret for his action.

It seems that Emilia had somehow been able to get her wish to be reborn as a man – as her own brother Paulo – but ultimately this had proved to be no more satisfying than her previous life and she chose self-destruction, just as she had done before, to end her misery. This case is not unique, for it seems that such traits and tendencies are likely to appear over a number of lifetimes, perhaps until the soul learns how to cope with problems and overcome them, rather than allowing them to bring down the curtain on life.

Professor Ian Stevenson has noted that in several cases in which the related previous personality had committed suicide, 'the subject has shown an inclination to contemplate and threaten suicide.'

WHO KILLED JOHN CISKO?

Among the Tlingit Indians of south-eastern Alaska, there is a strong belief not only in reincarnation but in rebirth into the same family. Such a case is that of Jimmy Svenson, whose father Olaf was half-Tlingit and half-Norwegian, and whose mother Millie was a full-blooded Tlingit.

Jimmy Svenson was born in Sitka on 22 November 1952 and within two years was claiming to be his mother's brother – John Cisko – and stating accurately that he had lived in the village of Klukwan, 100 miles (160 kilometres) away. Sometimes he would ask to go there to stay with his maternal grandmother. For two or three years Jimmy made many references to his previous life but then these diminished, as happens with the vast majority of children who have past-life memories.

John Cisko had been typical of the Tlingit tribe. He enjoyed hunting and fishing and consumed large quantities of alcohol, usually wine. During the summer of 1950, when he was twenty-five, John Cisko was in the army but had returned to Alaska on leave. One day he took a pleasure trip in a small fishing boat with two women and was never seen again. The bodies of the two women were found near the upright boat on a shore. They had drowned and the boat's bilge plug was missing, leading investigators to assume that the boat had filled with water rapidly, without its presumably inebriated occupants realising the danger until it was too late. Tides run high and currents swift in the channels of south-eastern Alaska and it seemed likely that John Cisko's body had been carried away rapidly on the ebbing tide. But there was also the possibility that he had been murdered, perhaps by a jealous lover of his two female companions.

So, does the testimony of Jimmy Svenson shed any light on the way in which he met his death?

When still a child, Jimmy told his parents that he had been shot to death 'by the skipper ... in the stomach'. Strangely, he was born with four circular marks on his stomach which Professor Stevenson examined in 1961 when the boy was nine years old – and by which time his past-life memories had totally faded. He writes:

They were about a quarter inch in diameter and clearly demarcated from the surrounding skin. Three had less pigment than the surrounding skin; one had somewhat more pigment. Three were along the line of the right lower ribs anteriorly, overlying the liver; the fourth was about two inches to the right of the umbilicus. The marks closely resembled healed bullet wounds of entry.

The appearance of birthmarks and birth defects coinciding with wounds suffered in a previous life can offer an additional physical means of corroborating reincarnation cases (and this is discussed in Chapter 20). In this case, however, there was a problem. There was no bullet-ridden body of John Cisko to prove the story; only the rumour of a witness who refused to speak, and a small boy who insisted that he was his own uncle and that he had been shot to death.

THE MAN WHO WAS BORN BEFORE HE DIED

Many years before the birth of Jimmy Svenson, researcher Francis Story recorded the experience of a Thai monk, the Venerable Phra Rajsuthajarn of Changwad Surin who belonged to the Pa Yodhaprasiddhi monastery in Thailand. Like Jimmy Svenson, he could remember a previous life in which his present mother had been his sister. In other words, his present grandparents had previously been his parents. What makes the story of Phra Rajsuthajarn so intriguing, however, is that he was born on 12 October 1908 – the day *before* the death of the man he remembered being. Such idiosyncrasies in reincarnation accounts remind us that, however compelling the evidence for rebirth, we are still a long way from understanding the mechanics of the spiritual laws which govern its operation.

When Phra Rajsuthajarn was old enough to speak he began recalling his previous life in considerable detail. He called his grandmother 'mother' and the three women who had been his daughters by their proper names – including one by her nickname as a baby. He also became angry when they would not call him 'father'.

In his former life as a farmer named Leng, Phra Rajsuthajarn had learned to speak Laotian and to read holy Buddhist scriptures in Cambodian characters. In his present life he found he could read Cambodian manuscripts without having learned the language, even though its alphabet is quite different from the Siamese. Despite having had no opportunity to learn Laotian in this life he was able to talk easily with people he met from Laos.

As Farmer Leng, Phra Rajsuthajarn had died at the age of forty-five from a fever. He could recall not only his former life but his death as well. He said he witnessed his own funeral rites, saw his body on the veranda and watched its cremation. During this time, he said, he had a wholly new kind of existence in which he felt he was able to 'see in all directions'. The day before Leng's death his younger sister had given birth to a son. Now, from the vantage point of the next world, he recalled going to his sister's side and looking down at the infant. He felt great affection and wanted to touch the child but held back for fear of disturbing it. Suddenly, he recalled, he had the sensation of falling and he was next aware of himself as the infant in the crib.

THE DANCING SISTERS

Another case involving reincarnation within the same family is reported from Finland. Six months separated the death of three-year-old Eeva-Maija Kaartinen from influenza in Helsinki and the birth of her sister Marja-Liisa on 22 May 1929. But it was not long before Salli Kaartinen realised that the daughter she had 'lost' had returned to her. It was Marja-Liisa who told her so. She even corrected strangers who called her Marja-Liisa. 'Eeva-Maija,' she would respond.

Dr Karl Müller, in his book, *Reincarnation – Based on Facts*, recorded the verbal testimony he had received from Mrs Kaartinen that her daughter was able to recognise people she had never seen before in this life and call them by their correct names. She also knew which clothes and toys had been hers in her previous life.

On one occasion, Mrs Kaartinen added, she had told Marja-Liisa: 'Mother is going to teach you some nursery songs which Eeva-Maija used to sing, and nicely too.' Then, as she began playing the piano, Marja-Liisa said: 'But Eeva-Maija also used to dance', and she began to dance the Charleston. Her mother had completely forgotten that, shortly before she died, her daughter had been taught by her cousins how to do the dance.

It does not seem unreasonable that a child who departs from this world at an early age might make another attempt at living with the same parents if the opportunity arises. There is even evidence that adults can make a similar choice – sometimes before they die.

THE WOMAN REBORN AS HER BROTHER'S DAUGHTER

Dr Sushil Chandra Bose records the story of a married woman named Betauli in his book, *Your Last Life and Your Next*. She used to say that in her next life she wanted to be the daughter of her brother Baburam and told his wife so. In 1908, the year when she made that statement, she died at Farrukhabad, India. Three years later, a daughter named Girija was born to her brother and his wife.

At the age of four Girija recognised her former father-in-law at a chance meeting and her former husband a year later. Seven years on, at the age of sixteen, she was taken to her former husband's house in Farukhabad, which she insisted was not her house. When taken to the old house she identified it immediately and pointed to where she used to sleep and cook the food. She also recognised Betauli's clothes, ornaments and a steel box she had used, and wept bitterly when she saw her former husband's second wife.

DEATH BY DROWNING

In one extraordinary case investigated by American researcher Dr Antonia Mills, the subject she interviewed was on his third incarnation with the same family in living memory. Emma Michell, a member of the Wet'suwet'en North American Indian tribe in British Columbia, was in her eighties when she supplied her evidence to Dr Mills. The past-life memories began when, many years earlier, her young nephew Jimmy heard the bell tolling in the small wooden church next door. He was told this was because a local man, Donald G., had died. Jimmy's response astonished his family: 'That's the one who hired men to beat me up and throw me in the river.'

The boy was apparently recalling the death of his uncle whose battered body had been dragged from the Bulkeley River before Jimmy was born. But history was to repeat itself, and Jimmy met his death in the same river. Now, say his family, he has returned for the third time and is Emma Michell's grandson who, as a child, had memories of both lives. He was heard to wish, as a child, that he had been a girl, since he would be less likely to meet another violent death in the waters of the turbulent river.

Such cases suggest that our soul's journey may not be such a lonely one after all. Perhaps those who are important to us in this life continue to play a significant role in our next existence.

During a visit to India in 1993 I met Indian researcher Dr Satwant Pasricha who, as well as conducting her own impressive investigations of reincarnation cases, has analysed the statistics recorded by her and others in the field. These reveal the prevalence of same-family reincarnation in certain cultures. For instance, she found a very high percentage of family links between Tlingits remembering a past life and the people they recalled being. In fact, this relationship was missing in only one case and was not known in four others, resulting in a 97.7 per cent association out of the total number of cases examined (47). A similar pattern of familial relationships emerged in three-quarters of the cases examined among the Haida (Indians of the Queen Charlotte Islands, British Columbia, and the southern part of Prince of Wales Island, Alaska). In Sri Lanka it was 16.7 per cent, in India 10.3 per cent and in Turkey 8.9 per cent.

These figures suggest that many families in these cultures may stay together over several lives.

chapter five

TWIN SOULS

THE MURDERED BOYS

It was only when three-year-old twin boys Ramoo and Rajoo Sharma ran away from the tiny village of Sham Nagara, Uttar Pradesh, India, in the direction of the railway station and main highway, that their parents realised there was something different about their sons. They were brought back and asked to explain what they were doing. Ramoo and Rajoo replied that they were 'going home'. It seems they were not asked to explain this remark but the truth was soon to emerge when an uncle saw them touching the feet of a stranger passing through their village (which is a way of expressing respect for someone you know). He reproached them because he knew they were not acquainted with this man. But they disagreed. They had recognised him, they explained, from their previous incarnation, and they began describing those lives in detail.

The boys, it emerged, had also been twins in their past lives. Ramoo had been Bhimsen Pitamah and Rajoo had been his brother Bhism. They had lived in the village of Uncha Larpur about 16 kilometres away – which is where the stranger in the street had come from – and they revealed that they had been murdered. What is more, they even identified their murderer, a man named Jagannath, with whom they had quarrelled, then later become apparently reconciled. His friendliness was a sham, however, and he invited them to his home in the village of Kurri, where a group of men attacked them and strangled them to death. They also described other events in their lives and objects they had owned.

There had indeed been twin boys named Pitamah who had

been murdered in the village of Kurri, and reports of their claims eventually filtered back to Uncha Larpur. As a result, members of their past-life family, other villagers and even the alleged murderers visited Sham Nagara to see Ramoo and Rajoo. Their visitors included the deceased twins' older brother, Chandra Sen, and their mother, Ram Devi, in the summer of 1971.

Shortly afterwards – on 20 November 1971 – Professor Ian Stevenson was in Gursahaiganj police station, Uttar Pradesh, enquiring about another case when a police officer suggested that he investigate the twins' story. Since it involved a murder not far away there were records in the police station which he was able to study. But he had no time to conduct personal enquiries on that occasion. Instead, he arranged for Dr L.P. Mehrotra to take statements from the principal witnesses in Sham Nagara and Uncha Larpur in July 1972. Professor Stevenson returned four months later to conduct further interviews and later Dr Erlendur Haraldsson also joined the investigation team.

Included in the evidence were court transcripts of the case against their alleged murderers, in which it was alleged that the Pitamah twins had been police informers. It was also revealed that a land dispute over boundaries had developed between them and two men named Jagannath and Raja Ram who successfully set a trap for the twins, who were last seen alive on 28 April 1964. Their bound and badly decomposed bodies were recovered from a well four days later and the police decided that they had been strangled.

'Suspicion naturally fell on the known enemies of the twins, and so the police rounded up a handful of these (in fact nine) and they were tried for the murders,' Professor Stevenson writes in Volume I of his *Cases Suggestive of Reincarnation*, dealing with India. 'But the murders had (almost certainly) been committed at night, and the police had probably netted all the eyewitnesses, so that no one remained to accuse them. For lack of direct evidence all the defendants were acquitted.'

Professor Stevenson considered going to Kurri to make further enquiries but decided that the prospects seemed 'so gloomy for meeting any person there who was not either one of the murderers or afraid of those who were, that I abandoned this expedition.'

Interestingly, Bhimsen and Bhism Pitamah had sons who also visited Sham Nagara. Ramoo and Rajoo called them 'sons', treated them paternally, and advised them to rebuild their home with proper care (it had decayed) and to visit Bhimsen's wife. When they met Ram Devi, their mother in their past life, they wept and so did she.

Although very different in personality, the twins were physically difficult to tell apart and were very close, even to the point of not eating a meal unless the other one was present. This closeness seems to have carried over from their past life, where, although they were both married with sons, they still did many things together, and indeed died together in a horrific way. In this life they have continued to be very close, even to the extent of talking as one and sharing the same memories of their previous incarnations.

It is worth noting, at this point, that India has provided a wealth of good reincarnation cases over the years and Professor Ian Stevenson has investigated most of them. Indeed, his very first book of case studies was concerned entirely with his Indian investigations, and he continues to return to that country to follow up new reports. His research, however, also takes him to Burma, Sri Lanka, Lebanon, Turkey and many other countries, including the United Kingdom. Living in the USA gives him easy access to North American cases, of course. And when I met him in London in 1996 I learned that he was planning a book of European case studies. The prevalence of Indian cases does not mean that reincarnation occurs more in that part of the world than it does elsewhere. A more plausible explanation seems to me that those cultures which accept rebirth are more likely to take note of children's claims to have lived before and accept them at face value, whereas in the West they would be dismissed as childish fantasy.

THE MARRIED COUPLE REBORN AS TWINS

Another carefully investigated case of twin boys who recall their past lives is equally impressive, though they were not even related in that earlier existence. Instead, they were a man and woman who lived in Okshitgon, Burma. The parents of Maung Gyi and Maung Ngé moved to Kabyu from Okshitgon shortly after they were born in 1886. The twins, therefore, had no knowledge of the place where they were born, nor of its inhabitants. Yet, as soon as they could speak, they began using different names for each other, one of which was a woman's. It was discovered that these were the names of a married couple who lived in Okshitgon and had been devoted to each other, having been born next door to each other on the same day. What is more, they had also died on the same day – at about the time the twins were born.

To test their past-life memories, Maung Gyi and Maung Ngé were taken to Okshitgon, to the home and neighbour-hood of the couple whose lives they recalled. They not only identified roads, places and people but also the clothes they had worn. The younger twin, who had been the wife, also remembered that she had borrowed two rupees from a Ma Thet which she had not repaid. When questioned, Ma Thet confirmed this. The man who investigated this case and wrote about it in *The Soul of a People*, Fielding Hall, interviewed the twins when they were six and still had strong memories of their former lives. The twin who remembered being the man was a chubby little fellow, whereas his brother was smaller and with 'a curious dreamy look in his face, more like a girl than a boy'.

'HE WAS MY COOK'

Even more curious is the past-life relationship of Krishnan Kishore who showed great affection for his twin brother Krishna Kumar and insisted on sharing everything with him. He gave him gifts and showed great concern for his well-being. When asked to explain his behaviour he replied, 'Because he was my cook.'

Eventually Krishnan told his mother that he did not relish the food she gave him because 'in my own house I used to get delicious sweets'. He went on to explain that he had owned a big red house, two cars and a gun, and had five sons all of whom were married. In that life his name had been Purushottom. The twins' uncle attempted to verify this story by taking Krishnan to a jeweller with that name but the boy did not recognise him. Later, his mother took him to the home of another Mr Purushottom and he was able to identify furniture, pictures and other items, even describing how they were obtained and what they were used for. It was also established during this visit that the late Mr Purushottom had owned cars and a gun and had been extraordinarily fond of sweets.

BURMESE TWINS

Professor Ian Stevenson, writing in *Children Who Remember Previous Lives*, tells us that his collection of cases suggestive of reincarnation contains thirty-six pairs of twins in whom one or both recalls a past life.

'In twenty-six of the cases of twin pairs a previous personality was satisfactorily identified for both twins', he says, adding that, in the others, one or both of the twins' cases remained unsolved – in other words, it was not possible to find evidence of the person they claimed to have been. 'Among the twenty-six solved cases, the previous personalities had had familial (sometimes marital) relationships in nineteen cases and had been friends or acquaintances in the remaining seven cases; in no instances had the previous personalities been strangers.'

Though not strangers, the relationship between Burmese twins Maung Aung Cho Thein and Maung Aung Ko Thein in their previous lives would, at first sight, have seemed an unlikely basis for them to be reborn in the same family. One had been a woman who owned a rice mill. The other was a farmer who took his rice to this mill. 'The behaviour of the twins toward each other reflected the somewhat haughty demeanour of the wealthy female mill owner and the deferential attitude of the paddy farmer,' Stevenson observes. 'We found this kind of dominant/submissive relationship in all eleven of the twin-pair cases for which we had sufficient information about the roles and behaviour of the subjects and previous personalities.'

Despite the tremendous efforts of researchers working in the field of reincarnation studies, it is not always possible to corroborate children's past-life memories and such cases, for obvious reasons, seldom feature in their reports or statistics. But Professor Stevenson makes an exception for Burmese twin girls Ma Khin San Tin and Ma Khin San Yin because of the remarkable similarity of their stories which emerged when he was conducting his research. The girls remembered being Japanese brothers (not twins) who had served in the same army unit. They died in Burma in April 1945 during the British advance near Pyawbwe. After that, they told him, they had tried to be reborn in Japan but had failed. So they returned to the place where they had died in Burma and were born in a village less than 100 metres from where they said they had been killed and where there had been a Japanese army entrenchment. 'This case remains unsolved,' Professor Stevenson reminds us, 'as do those of the other Burmese children claiming to have been Japanese soldiers killed in Burma.'

THE POLLOCK TWINS

An announcement in Northumberland's *Hexham Courant* in 1958 barely hinted at the remarkable story that was about to unfold. It read:

> POLLOCK. To John and Florence at 29 Leazes Crescent, Hexham, on October 4th, God's precious gift of twin daughters, Jennifer and Gillian Theresa. Thanks be to God and to our Blessed Lady.

The Pollock name would have been familiar to most of the English newspaper's readers, since it had featured prominently in its columns eighteen months earlier after fate tragically robbed John and Florence of their two daughters, Joanna, eleven, and Jacqueline, six. The girls walked from their home to St Mary's Church every Sunday, together with their friend Anthony Layden, to attend a special Mass held for the local Roman Catholic School's 250 pupils. But on 5 May 1957, they never reached the church. As the trio walked hand-in-hand along Shafto Leazes, a car, driven by a woman who had taken a drug overdose with the intention of taking her life, mounted the pavement and drove straight into them. The impact tossed them into the air like rag dolls and Joanna and Jacqueline died instantly from multiple injuries. Their nine-year-old friend was also found to be dead on arrival at hospital.

Though devastated by their loss, the Pollocks found it in their hearts to send the woman responsible for the tragedy a joint message of condolence and forgiveness. John Pollock was already a staunchly religious man – a Roman Catholic convert at the age of nineteen – and Florence, comforted by the kindness of their local priest, joined him soon after their daughters' death. But John was an unusual Roman Catholic for he also held a very strong belief in reincarnation – a view not shared by his wife. In fact, he had prayed at night for some proof of rebirth so that he could show the priests that he was right.

At first John Pollock viewed the death of Joanna and Jacqueline as God's judgement on him for praying for proof of reincarnation. But at the same time he decided that God intended to answer his prayers and that the girls would return to them. Again, this was not a belief which his wife shared and it put considerable pressure on her. So it was with some anxiety that she announced early the following year that she was pregnant. Her delighted husband responded with confidence that God was returning Joanna and Jacqueline to them and that she would give birth to twin girls. John Pollock now had not only his wife's disbelief to contend with but also the medical verdict of their doctor and a gynaecologist that there was only one child in the womb. Yet, miraculously, John Pollock's prediction was fulfilled and twin daughters Jennifer and Gillian were safely brought into the world, ten minutes apart.

Almost immediately their father noticed a thin white line running down the forehead of the youngest twin, Jennifer. He had seen a mark just like that before – on the forehead of Jacqueline. She had gashed her head at the age of two and the wound had healed to leave a thin white scar. Despite her scepticism, Florence Pollock noticed a brown birthmark on Jennifer's left hip which corresponded in size, shape and position to one which Jacqueline was born with. Since the twins were genetically identical (the medical term is monozygotic, meaning from a single egg cell) such a difference is very rare.

These physical signs were sufficient to convince John Pollock that his dead daughters had been reborn. He was soon to have even greater proof. They had decided to move to another part of Northumberland and they made their new home in Whitley Bay just four months after the birth of the twins. The girls were three years old when they made their first return visit to Hexham for a day, yet Gillian and Jennifer behaved as if they knew it well. As they walked along the street, their parents listened with fascination to their running commentary. 'The school's just around the corner,' said one of them, even though at that moment the school their sisters had attended was still hidden by the church. 'That's where we used to play in the playground,' said the other. Back came the response: 'The swings and slides are over there.' She nodded in the direction of a hill and her parents knew that their daughters *had* played on swings and slides which were out of sight on the other side of the hill. Then, as they passed the house in which Joanna and Jacqueline had spent many happy years, they both said: 'We used to live there.'

The Pollocks had kept their dead daughters' toys in cardboard boxes, unwilling to part with them. As their twins grew up they decided they should put the old toys to good use and so two old dolls and a toy clothes wringer were placed outside their bedroom door one night. It was Florence Pollock who watched their discovery. Jennifer was the first to see them. 'Oh, that's Mary. And this is my Suzanne,' she exclaimed, adding, 'I haven't seen her for a long time.' She then turned to her twin sister and said, 'And there's your wringer.' Jennifer had correctly named the dolls and attributed ownership of them and the wringer.

More chilling was their reaction, while playing at the rear of their house in Whitley Bay near a lane in which cars were parked. Hearing hysterical screaming one day, John Pollock rushed out to find the twins locked in each other's arms, crouched in a corner, repeating, 'The car! The car! it's coming at us!' They were pointing towards a car which was facing them and which had just started ... a scene which must have been reminiscent of that which presented itself in Joanna and Jacqueline's final moments. Even more macabre was Gillian and Jennifer's apparent re-enactment of their death which their mother witnessed in their playroom when they were not aware that they were being observed. Gillian was cradling her younger twin's head in her hands and saying, 'The blood's coming out of your eyes. That's where the car hit you.'

Soon after that the twins' memories began to fade and by the time they reached their twenties they could recall nothing about any of these incidents.

In examining reincarnation in families, we have to be wary of the influence, deliberate or otherwise, of parents or other relatives who may impose their own beliefs on impressionable children. This works both ways, however, for there are many cases where it is obvious that a child's apparent past-life memories have been unwelcome and therefore silenced by punishment or threats. We must also consider how much of what is apparently remembered could be the result of 'genetic memory' – even though there is no scientific proof that memory is something which can be handed down from one generation to another.

One of the best accounts of the Pollock family's experiences appears in Ian Wilson's *Mind Out of Time* which was published as a paperback under the title *Reincarnation?*. This book is highly critical of reincarnation reports in general, suggesting that most researchers are not fastidious enough in checking their subjects' testimony. But Ian Wilson, who now lives in Australia and is one of my magazine's correspondents, concedes that the case of the Pollock Twins may be exceptional. He says this of John Pollock and his daughters: '... if

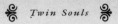

everything happened the way he has described, including the twins' reliving of their dead sisters' memories, then I have to recognise that something not yet within the understanding of twentieth-century science would seem to have been at work.'

chapter six

SOULMATES

THE PHARAOH'S LOVER

Visitors to Abydos, one of ancient Egypt's most important archaeological sites, in the 1970s, were often shown around the beautiful Temple of Sety I by an apparently eccentric Englishwoman with an immense knowledge of the place and the man who built it.

Dorothy Eady's expertise can be explained in part by her long association with eminent Egyptologists, her ability to translate hieroglyphics and her work for Egypt's Antiquities Department on various restoration projects, including sites close to the Great Pyramid at Giza. But she also offered insights into the daily lives of the Egyptians and their rituals which puzzled the experts and earned her even greater respect when evidence was uncovered to prove her right. Her explanation was simple: she knew these things because she had lived there before, in the time of Sety I.

However, behind this claim was an even more astonishing story and one which even some believers in reincarnation might find hard to accept. Dorothy Eady believed that she and Pharaoh Sety I had been lovers in that life and were soulmates destined to be together for all eternity if she could pass certain tests which would present themselves in this life. She was certain that the great pharaoh, Sety I, had been searching for her from the next world for 3,000 years and eventually found her when she was a teenager living in Plymouth, Devon. He appeared to her and, having re-established the relationship which had ended so many years earlier, they began a two-world liaison which was to take her back to Abydos, 325 miles (520 kilometres) south of Cairo, to live and die in the romantic shadow of that earlier love affair.

There is nothing in Dorothy Eady's family history or child-hood to explain her love of Egypt, which manifested itself soon after she fell down a flight of steps in 1907 at her home in Blackheath, south-east London. She was three years old … and was declared dead by the family doctor. When he returned later with a nurse to wash and lay out the child's body he found Dorothy sitting up in bed, her face smeared with choco-late, happily playing.

Soon after that incident she began having recurring dreams of a huge building with columns and a garden filled with fruit and flowers. Her parents would frequently find her weeping. When asked why, she would tell them, 'I want to go home', though she did not know where 'home' was. When she was taken to the British Museum at the age of four, she ran with delight through the Egyptian galleries, kissing all the statues. Eventually she settled quietly, transfixed by a mummy, refusing to leave when it was time to go. Her mother stooped to pick her up but the child grabbed hold of the glass case and said in an eerie voice, like that of a strange, old woman: 'Leave me … *these* are my people.' She was carried, kicking and screaming, from the museum.

She would pore over pictures of the Rosetta Stone with a magnifying glass and when asked why, since she did not know the language, she responded: 'I *do* know it, but I've just forgotten it. If I could only copy it down, perhaps I might remember it.'

At the age of seven Dorothy saw, in a magazine brought home by her father, a photograph whose caption read: 'The Temple of Sety I at Abydos, Upper Egypt'. She ran to her father excitedly, declaring, '*This* is my home! *This* is where I used to live! … But why is it all broken? And where is the garden?'

Reuben Eady scolded her for telling lies and explained that it was broken because it was very old and there was no garden because it was in the middle of the desert. He became even more annoyed with his daughter when she told him, on seeing a picture of Sety I's well-preserved mummy, which is in the Cairo Museum, that she knew this man and he was good and kind. She must stop all this nonsense once and for all, he demanded.

His words were wasted on Dorothy who, as she grew up, began taking days off school in order to visit the British Museum and spend time among the relics of ancient Egypt. There she met Sir E.A. Wallis Budge, the Keeper of Egyptian and Assyrian Antiquities, who taught her to read hieroglyphics. And eventually she met and married an Egyptian who took her back to Cairo to live. The marriage lasted only three years – Imam Abdel Meguid had no idea when they wed that he would be competing with a dead pharaoh for his wife's love – but they produced a son who Dorothy insisted must be named Sety. After they divorced she continued to live in Egypt, working on various archaeological projects, and as is customary there she became known as 'Omm Sety', which means 'Mother of Sety'.

In the 1950s the Antiquities Department finally agreed to her persistent request for a transfer from Cairo to Abydos. It was not a post the department would normally have filled with a woman, since the village in which she had to live had no electricity, plumbing or running water. But Omm Sety was delighted. She had come home. What is more, during the temple's restoration, workmen found the garden she had seen in her dreams, 'exactly where I said it was – to the south-west of the temple – tree roots, vine roots, little channels for watering … even the well; and the well *still* had water in it.'

During her time in Cairo, the full story of her previous life in Egypt, she revealed later, was 'dictated' to her by someone called Hor-Ra who made intermittent visits at night, from the next world. It took a year to complete and when translated ran to seventy pages. From this, Omm Sety learned that she had been a golden-haired, blue-eyed fourteen-year-old girl named Bentreshyt who was noticed by the pharaoh during a visit to Abydos to oversee the construction of the monumental shrine being erected for him. They fell in love and met clandestinely because Bentreshyt was a virgin priestess of Isis and was therefore temple property. Nobody was allowed to touch her, not even the pharaoh.

It soon became apparent, however, that Bentreshyt was pregnant and the high priest Antef forced her to confess to her crime and eventually name her lover. Death was the only possible sentence for her crime but it also called for a public trial. Rather than have her lover's name revealed in public, Bentreshyt took her own life. Pharaoh Sety I, who had gone on a trip to Numia, was shocked and heartbroken to learn what had happened on his return to Abydos and vowed never to forget her. And, it seems, he never did.

The most extraordinary aspect of the Omm Sety story is that, throughout her work on Egypt's ancient monuments, the Englishwoman claimed that she and Sety I were meeting regularly – sometimes on the astral plane and occasionally in her own home where he would materialise, lie beside her on the bed and even make love to her. This physical relationship had to end when she transferred to Abydos, however, and he told her: 'The chariot wheel of fate has turned its full circle. From now until the end of your earthly life you belong again to the temple, and you are forbidden to me or to any man.' Omm Sety began to cry and the pharaoh consoled her by asking if she was going to make the same mistake all over again.

'Then he explained to me that this was the period in which we were both to be tested. If we resisted temptation for the rest of my life in Abydos, our original crime would be forgiven, and I would belong to him for eternity.'

Dorothy Eady knew that few people would believe her story, so she kept a secret diary of these other-world meetings, and confided only in her closest friends, including Dr Hanny El Zeini, president of the Sugar and Distillery Company of Egypt. He collaborated with Jonathan Cott to produce the remarkable book of her life, *The Search for Omm Sety*, which appeared in 1988, more than six years after her death.

Omm Sety died as she wished and is buried close to the temple where she claimed to have died once before in her life as Bentreshyt.

It has to be said that the story of Omm Sety raises more questions than it answers. If Dorothy Eady really had been Bentreshyt, the lover of Sety I, in her previous life, why did it take 3,000 years for them to discover each other? Did Dorothy Eady have other incarnations in the intervening period? Or was her soul in some form of suspended animation, waiting for the right set of circumstances to allow their reunion to take place?

I have no answers to these questions. Indeed, the whole subject of soulmates is fraught with difficulty. Yet the idea that we each have a partner ('our other half') without whom we are incomplete, is a powerful concept for those who believe in reincarnation. It also surfaces, of course, in great literature and poetry. Many couples testify that, when they first met their partner, it felt like a reunion: as if they had been together before. Taken at face value, this suggests that, over the centuries and in many lifetimes, among the many souls with whom we form relationships, we are drawn to one in particular with whom our destiny is inextricably bound. Though we are most likely to become lovers, we may have to experience other relationships with that soul in order to help our mutual understanding. Nor will time spent with our soulmate always be happy: some of these lifetimes may be difficult and painful.

HELPING SOULMATES CONNECT

Dr Brian Weiss is a firm believer in soulmates and reincarnation. A graduate of Columbia University and Yale Medical School in the United States, he now lives and practises as a psychiatrist in Miami, Florida. 'I have worked with many people, usually couples, who have found themselves together in previous lives,' he explains. 'Many have recognised their soul companions, travelling together through time to be united once again in the current lifetime.'

But all his years of regressing people back to their former lives did not prepare him for an extraordinary dilemma involving two of his patients who, under hypnosis, appeared to have been related in their previous existences but did not know each other in this.

Pedro, a Mexican who sought Dr Weiss's help after the death of his brother, described one life in which Roman soldiers tied him to their horses and dragged him along the ground, then had a game with him in which he struck his head on a rock. They left him to die in the arms of his daughter.

Elizabeth, a tall and successful businesswoman, sought Dr Weiss's help after reading one of his books because she felt her life was a mess. When regressed, she described a past life in which she was Miriam whose father died in her arms after being dragged behind Roman soldiers' horses.

Pedro and Elizabeth (pseudonyms given by Weiss to ensure his patients' privacy) had a series of sessions with Dr Weiss over many months. They booked on different days and were strangers to each other. Nor did the psychiatrist notice the similarities in their accounts, during which they appeared to be playing different roles in the same scenes. Then, towards the very end of their treatment, Dr Weiss examined their notes and became convinced that they were destined for each other.

'Never before had I encountered soulmates who had not yet met in the present time,' he writes in his book *Only Love Is Real*. 'In this case, soulmates who had travelled nearly 2,000 years to be together again. They had come all this way. They were within inches and minutes of each other, but they had not yet connected.'

What should he do? 'I was severely constrained by the "laws" of psychiatry, if not the more subtle rules of karma,' he explains. To breach patient confidentiality could constitute malpractice. But Pedro was planning to move back to Mexico. 'If Pedro and Elizabeth did not meet soon, they would be in different countries, and the likelihood of their meeting in this lifetime would be dramatically diminished.'

Dr Weiss' solution was to arrange their appointments back-to-back so that, as Pedro left a consultation, he would meet Elizabeth in the waiting room. They met. They looked at each other. And they parted. 'My manipulation had been too subtle, too fleeting,' he writes, adding, 'Fortunately, minds more creative than mine were expertly conspiring from lofty heights to arrange a meeting between Elizabeth and Pedro. The reunion was predestined. What happened afterwards would be up to them.'

Pedro went to the airport to begin the first stage of his

journey back to Mexico. Elizabeth had gone there, too, at a different time, to take a flight to an important business appointment. Her aircraft was delayed, however, because of mechanical failure and she was transferred to the same flight as Pedro. They recognised each other in the departure hall and diffidently started talking. Soon they were arranging to move seats so that they could sit together on the aircraft, and when it ran into turbulence Pedro reached out to hold her hand. 'Elizabeth could feel lifetimes being awakened by the current.'

Dr Brian Weiss still hears from Pedro and Elizabeth. They are now happily married and living in Mexico with a beautiful daughter.

Though he played a minor role in the match-making, the psychiatrist advises: 'Never worry about meeting soulmates. Such meetings are a matter of destiny. They *will* occur. After the meeting, the free will of both partners reigns … When allowed to flow freely, love overcomes all obstacles.'

BORN TO BE TOGETHER

Best-selling author Jess Stearn is a world-renowned authority on spirituality and reincarnation whose books include *Edgar Cayce: The Sleeping Prophet*, *Yoga, Youth and Reincarnation*; and *Soulmates*, which illustrates the concept of unlimited, unconditional, unending love with various examples, including celebrities such as Shirley MacLaine, Susan Strasberg and Howard Hughes.

Among the case studies, however, is an unusual one. Dick Sutphen has done more than most to promote the idea of reincarnation, writing sixteen metaphysical books, giving lectures, holding seminars and conducting past-life regression sessions in which individuals can explore what appear to be memories of previous existences. 'In all my work in this area,' he told Jess Stearn, 'I have found only a few cases where I have been unable to establish a past link between present lovers.'

Amplifying on this idea, he added: 'Relationships and the concept of destiny manipulating us on the chessboard of life have always been my primary interest. I know that shared past lives are the prerequisite for an important relationship in this life. People appear to come together by an unseen plan.'

But Sutphen himself appeared to be having difficulty finding his own soulmate. He had been married three times, with many relationships in between, and was in the middle of his third divorce when Jess Stearn invited him to a party at his home. Another guest was Tara McKean, twenty years younger than Dick Sutphen and also going through a divorce. There was an immediate, mutual attraction.

Dick Sutphen decided to explore his own past incarnations to see if he and Tara had shared a life together. Meditating at Sedona, Arizona, he saw himself walking down a path with a beautiful woman, who he knew was Tara, to a circular area overlooking a bay. In that life, he discovered, he wanted to go off to take up an important assignment. She, however, wanted him to remain under the protection of her wealthy parents. Tearfully, they agreed to part. Later, looking at a map of South America, Dick identified the place where this past life parting occurred: at Maracaibo in Venezuela.

Tara, who had never been regressed to a past life before, agreed to allow Dick to hypnotise her and she described exactly the same scene. She also recalled earlier lives together, back to prehistoric times, when 'I carried his spear and we made love. But I didn't love him. I never loved him.'

They also sought a past-life reading with a well-known psychic, Alan Vaughan, who told them they had lived together in Mongolia (where the sex roles were reversed, Tara being the man and Dick the woman), Rome, Mexico, Nova Scotia and, finally, South America where he described a very similar scene to that seen by Dick and Tara in their own past-life recollections.

Since then, the couple have grown very close. Tara now declares, 'I truly love him,' adding, 'Everything I am tells me we are finally together at the right time and place.' To which Dick adds, 'This time, it's forever.'

Having met in Jess Stearn's home at Malibu, California, they asked also to be married there, on 2 March 1984, over-looking the blue Pacific.

'I had never seen Tara more beautiful,' Stearn writes in *Soulmates*. 'But now, with the gleam in her eyes, and the

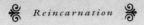

answering glow in Richard's, as they became Mr and Mrs Richard Sutphen, they had finally achieved the fulfilment that had eluded them through all their misadventures.'

Their union has since been blessed with two children – Cheyenne and Hunter – and the couple work together promoting reincarnation and the concept of soulmates, by teaching and example. In that work, as we will see in the next chapter, they have the support of a large number of people who have pledged to be reborn in order to champion the concept of reincarnation.

chapter seven

GROUP
REINCARNATION

BURIED ALIVE

Dick Sutphen, the world-famous Californian past-life regressionist and lecturer, believes an event that happened over 1,400 years ago has been responsible for motivating and directing him in this life. What is more, he says he is one of 25,000 people who, in AD 581–582, in Mexico, made a pact to be reborn every 700 years to ensure that their belief in reincarnation and other metaphysical concepts was not lost to the human race.

The setting for this dramatic past-life memory was Teotihuacán, 'the City of the Gods', in pre-Columbian central Mexico, some 33 miles (53 kilometres) north of modern Mexico City. After four centuries of growth, Teotihuacán started to become a major metropolis around the same time as the birth of Christianity. At its height, its 8 square miles (21 square kilometres) contained homes, plazas, temples and palaces. A single 1½-mile (2.4 kilometre) road, the Avenue of the Dead, connected the Pyramid of the Moon and associated buildings, at the north end of the city, with the Temple of Quetzalcóatl, to the south. To the east was the great Pyramid of the Sun. Teotihuacán was a massive conurbation. Bigger than Imperial Rome, it housed over 200,000 inhabitants. Yet mystery still surrounds its rulers, for there are no records of their names or achievements. And after perhaps a thousand years of peace and prosperity the city of Teotihuacán suffered a major disaster: it was sacked, burned and partially destroyed.

Archaeologists are still trying to piece together the history of Teotihuacán but Dick Sutphen believes that some of its past has already unfolded before his eyes, in a psychic vision, and other clues to its downfall have been revealed by a voice in his head. It sounds unlikely, but Sutphen has files of letters from other Americans who have responded to his past-life regressions and helped him uncover the truth of the ordeal they all suffered.

He tells the full story in his book *Earthly Purpose*. However, because there were so many gaps in his knowledge which even his correspondents were unable to answer, Dick Sutphen fictionalised part of the account in order to help the story flow. He invented names for the main protagonists and brought the account to life by reporting details and speech that are clearly invented. To make matters worse, from the sceptics' point of view, his leading characters are hooded figures from Atlantis with blue, glowing rods of crystal which can exert tremendous power (shades of *Star Wars*!). But Dick Sutphen is certain it all happened much as he describes.

Sutphen believes that the powers of evil, represented by the religion of the Jaguar, decided to replace the existing religion in Teotihuacán which was one of love and light. As the soldiers approached, he says, Xrote the Elder told his followers:

> No one can control you as long as you accept what you know to be so. No matter what the outcome of this battle, the oppressor cannot touch our souls. We will return. We can choose to return together, to carry the torch of light as a shared goal. Let it be every seven hundred years.

The crowd of 25,000 people echoed his cry, over and over. Later, thirty-five priests (including Sutphen in his previous incarnation), and at least 200 supporters, were captured and marched out of the city to a newly dug pit. There they were made to stand overnight and a further 100 people were thrown in the next day. Then the leader of the Jaguar religion, Khatic, arrived and sneered contemptuously, 'If you're coming back in seven hundred years, I'll swear on my father's grave I'll be there as well.' So the battle between good and evil is apparently destined to continue and believers in reincarnation can always expect to face opposition. With that, he commanded the soldiers to bury his opponents alive.

It's a storyline so awful that one feels it must either be true or written with the hope of selling it as a Hollywood block-buster. But before we scoff, we should consider other cases of group reincarnation which also suggest that large numbers of people *do* reincarnate with a purpose.

THE REBORN CATHARS

The question Dick Sutphen does not attempt to answer is what this group of souls did 700 years ago, when they were supposed to have been reborn to keep their pledge for the first time. Perhaps the first person to write at any length about group reincarnation, Arthur Guirdham, an Oxford scholar, doctor of medicine, psychiatrist, scientist and philosopher, may have had the answer. Many of his writings concern events which happened between 700 and 800 years ago, at around the time Sutphen and his group should have been honouring their pledge.

Born in 1905, Guirdham won the Governor's Clinical Gold Medal at Charing Cross Hospital, London, in 1929 and was a senior consultant psychiatrist in the Bath area of Somerset for over thirty years. He would not have found Dick Sutphen's account of the sinister overtones behind the Teotihuacán massacre difficult to accept, for Guirdham also saw the world as being involved in a cosmic battle between good and evil. He was equally certain that we all live many lives.

But the concept of group reincarnation was forced upon him in middle age when a woman patient, whom he called Mrs Smith, confided in him about her strange experiences. These included having detailed psychic knowledge of Catharism, the heretical belief in dualism which was popular in southern France and northern Italy between seven and eight centuries earlier. She also discovered that parts of France were familiar to her, particularly St Jean Pied de Port which she visited for the first time on holiday in the 1960s and around which she was able to find her way as if it were her home town. At Toulouse and particularly in its cathedral, on the other hand, she felt horror. It was there that many Cathars were tried and found guilty of heresy.

Guirdham was at first impatient with Mrs Smith's accounts, which he regarded as fantasies, even though he himself had also been strangely attracted to France, particularly Languedoc and the Pyrenees. Then she described to him a recurring nightmare in which she was filled with terror as a man entered her room and came towards her from the right. This struck a chord with the Bath psychiatrist for he, too, was suffering from an almost identical nightmare, in which a man came towards him from the left. She knew that the person in her dream had committed a murder and was unrepentant. What she kept from Guirdham at their first meeting – and for a long time afterwards – was the fact that she also recognised Guirdham as her Cathar lover, Roger Isarn.

There quickly followed a series of coincidences, including two women telling him that they were certain he had been a Cathar in a previous life, which compelled Guirdham to look more deeply into Mrs Smith's claims. As a result of the information she supplied and his subsequent research he became convinced that the unrepentant murderer in their nightmares was Pierre de Mazarolles, a well-known Cathar identified as one of the murderers of the Inquisitors who largely succeeded in wiping out the dualist heresy.

It is a complicated story, which Guirdham, who died in 1992, told in his book, *The Cathars and Reincarnation*. But it is one which sceptics find difficult to dismiss without calling upon fraud or some psychic explanation for the names and other material which came to the main people involved, including Guirdham. Much of this information was not readily accessible at that time. For example, in 1944 Mrs Smith had described the Cathars as wearing dark blue robes. Experts would have dismissed this as inaccurate at the time because they were certain that Cathar robes were black, but evidence came to light twenty-one years later that Cathar robes were in fact dark blue.

The English psychiatrist became convinced that he and a

group of people who now knew each other had lived and died together as Cathars. He extended this claim in his other books, such as *The Lake and the Castle* and *We Are One Another*, in which another subject, a Miss Mills, also provided a wealth of information about Catharism by psychic means. Slowly, other people came forward who also appeared to be reborn members of the group.

To get a full appreciation of the Arthur Guirdham story one needs to read all his books, but the best summary of them appears in David Christie-Murray's excellent and level-headed *Reincarnation: Ancient Beliefs and Modern Evidence*. He writes:

> If group reincarnation is not acceptable as an explanation, some other must be found. It is difficult to see what normal psychological interpretation can be suggested. The string of coincidences and relationships is too bizarre to be explained by chance, yet the recorded facts will fit no ordinary hypothesis. Guirdham wrote: 'The whole experience has become so oceanic that I can now do little more than record it'.

A TRIBE RETURNED

A similar feeling was almost certainly experienced by Janet Cunningham, a United States therapist whose early work with overweight patients led her to the discovery that this condition usually had a past-life cause. Then she became caught up in the memories and psychic experiences of people from various parts of America who appeared to be recalling lives as Native American Indians who had been massacred by white soldiers. And she, it transpired, was a key figure in the violent drama that unfolded, despite her efforts to remain an objective observer.

This group regression, she believes, had a purpose. Those she regressed to that shared past-life, when they were all members of the Oglala tribe in the Dakotas, have been reborn together in the twentieth century in order to heal themselves of the suffering they endured in that earlier existence. They have been reborn together only as far as time is concerned: geographically, many of the group live far from each other but have been drawn to Janet Cunningham and her work.

For her part, the past-life therapist says she was careful not to ask leading questions during hypnosis sessions. Nor did she divulge to others what was said, even when they were describing the same events or recognising each other in their past-life memories. Eventually the reborn members of the tribe sat down together as a group and recalled the grisly details of that tragic event. It's an emotional story which clearly had a great impact on all those involved, not least the author.

Janet Cunningham reveals somewhat reluctantly in her book, *A Tribe Returned*, that in that incarnation she had been Falling Star, daughter of the tribe's leader, Silver Eagle. She met her death at the age of fourteen after being raped by the soldiers. They then cut out her heart and gave it to her father. Her sons and her estranged husband in this life, it transpires, were also members of the tribe. And, as if that were not enough to cope with, she adds that the white soldiers who were their murderers are now married to some of the members of the tribe they massacred in order to work out their guilt.

Those caught up in this rebirth drama have no doubts about its authenticity, though Janet Cunningham endeavours to retain her objectivity to the very end. She admits that she does not know whether it is true because she has not been able to uncover any evidence that the massacre of the Oglala tribe occurred.

'Could we have tapped into each other's unconscious minds and created a metaphor?' she asks. 'Perhaps. Or – maybe – we are a tribe that has returned.'

THE TOWN THAT REINCARNATED

Coincidentally, another past-life therapist also produced a book about group reincarnation shortly before Janet Cunningham's appeared. In this, Marge Rieder claimed that, under hypnosis, fifty residents of the same American town were all able to remember living before, together, in a small town of which they had never previously heard.

Her story begins with journalist Maureen Williamson's visit to Lake Elsinore, California, in November 1986. She called at a café where she ordered a slice of carrot cake and wrote down the name John Daniel Ashford. Both actions were puzzling for she hated carrot cake and did not know anyone by that name.

Later, under hypnosis, she told Marge Rieder that her name had been Becky and Ashford had been her husband during the American Civil War when they had lived at Millboro in the state of Virginia. Neither had heard of Millboro but they eventually found it on the map. At a later session, Becky revealed that Maureen's boss in this life, Barbara Roberts, had been her mother-in-law at Millboro. Barbara agreed to be hypnotised and, sure enough, she described the small town in very similar terms to Becky.

So, were there any other residents of Lake Elsinore who had previously lived in Millboro? 'Yes,' Becky answered, to the hypnotherapist's astonishment, 'there were fifty.' Among them was private investigator Joe Nazarowski whose wife was a friend of Maureen's. Becky remembered him as Charley Morgan and he, too, agreed to be regressed. Under hypnosis Joe Nazarowski revealed that he had been a Confederate soldier sent to Millboro as a secret agent to destroy a railway tunnel. He met Becky – by then the mother of eight – and they had an affair. Although her husband fought for the North, incidentally, Becky was on the side of the South, as was Charley Morgan.

But their affair led to tragedy when she was strangled in front of her children by a villain called Jake Bauer.

The full story, with photographs of many of the people involved, is told in Marge Rieder's book, *Mission to Millboro*, but she admits that despite many other items of corroboratory evidence (some of which are discussed in Chapter 19), the author and the others involved in this group reincarnation have so far found no evidence that John Ashford, Becky or her mother-in-law once lived in Millboro. Nor are there any records of Becky's murder or Jake's hanging.

Marge Rieder insists that, whatever the explanation, her subjects are not remembering information absorbed earlier in this life and forgotten (a phenomenon known as cryptomnesia). All but two of the subjects had never even heard of Millboro, she says; nor had they been to Virginia when the research started. One theory offered to explain the failure to find three of the leading characters is that the records were altered to cover up the murder. Sceptics would argue, however, that there is a simpler explanation: it never happened.

In her attempts to unravel the mystery, Marge Rieder used some interesting techniques, including simultaneous regression of several people to describe their symbiotic relationships, and walking hypnosis, in which the subject sees two timeframes, past and present, superimposed on each other.

THE RETURN OF THE JAPANESE SAMURAI

A group reincarnation of a very different kind was discovered by Alex Weeks, an English therapist, during a research project with gay men who are HIV positive. He approached me to ask if his preliminary findings, based on 300 past-life memories of fifty gay men, could be published in *Reincarnation International Magazine*. He knew that it would be easy for the more sensational members of the media to twist his research results and jump to false conclusions, whereas we would treat them impartially and encourage others to carry out similar work in an attempt to replicate his results. As a gay man who is also a Tibetan Buddhist, Alex Weeks explained, his primary aim in conducting the research was a spiritual one.

For some time he had been concerned that writers on reincarnation often took the view that gay men were women imprisoned in a male body. He did not believe this but realised that there had not been enough serious research in this area to say so with any certainty. His research project took five years and, he claims, shows 'very clear trends' involving gay men with Aids. These trends, he says, are 'beginning to become startlingly consistent'.

The most thought-provoking trend concerns a cohort of people – a term used to describe a group of people who have a connection or, in scientific terms, are part of a study.

According to Alex Weeks, these people:

> appear to have had Samurai warrior connections and have
> blood connections and that sort of thing. There's a very
> definite connection between nine or ten people who are
> not known to each other who are talking about *exactly*
> the same place in Japan, in the *same circumstances* and in
> the *same time* in history: the 13th century.

Alex Weeks' research continues and he is cautious about
jumping to conclusions. But he makes this observation: 'It
does appear, as far as gay men and Aids are concerned, that
there are groups of people who are drawn together and appear
to reincarnate together.'

chapter eight

LOOKING FOR REBORN LAMAS

WHERE THE PEACH TREE BLOOMS

The best-known reincarnation in the world is, of course, the Dalai Lama – Tibet's spiritual and political leader who now lives in exile in India since the Chinese invasion of his country. After his death in each life, his followers embark upon a search for him, based on a curious mixture of psychic portents and scientific objectivity. It is believed that he is currently in his fourteenth incarnation. The Dalai Lama, himself, uses his own intuitive powers, as well as the services of oracles, to confirm the reincarnation of other eminent lamas in Tibetan Buddhism. And in his last life he seems to have given an extraordinary intimation of where he would be reborn.

It happened soon after the Thirteenth Dalai Lama died, in 1933. His body sat in state in Lhasa's Potala Palace, home of the Dalai Lamas for centuries, in the traditional Buddha posture, looking south. One morning, however, it was noticed that his head had miraculously turned to the east. The state oracle was consulted and, while in trance, threw a white scarf in the direction of the rising sun, confirming that the Fourteenth Dalai Lama would be born in the east. Part of the divination process in the search for him involved visiting Lhamo Namtso, a sacred lake, and looking into its deep, blue waters in order to see visions that would provide clues to his whereabouts.

The young regent who had this responsibility saw in the lake a vision of a three-storey monastery with roofs of gold and copper. There was a twisting road leading to a mountain and a Chinese-style peasant building of moderate size, with distinctive carved gables painted blue. Nearby was a peach tree in bloom and a woman with a baby in her arms. This image was duly recorded and placed under seal so that it could not be tampered with – an approach that would please any self-respecting investigator of rebirth cases today. In fact, such scientific procedures had been in place for several hundred years in Tibet, since the early days of the Dalai Lama lineage, which began with the birth of Gedun Truppa in 1391.

Three groups consisting of monks and at least one secular state official then began to search the country east of Lhasa, the direction to which the Thirteenth Dalai Lama's head had turned. With them they took articles that had belonged to their leader, as well as some which did not – again with the laudable aim of determining whether any apparent reincarnation of the Dalai Lama could differentiate between the two.

The search continued for a considerable time until one of the three groups arrived at Jye-kun-do, home of the Panchen Lama, one of Tibetan Buddhism's most revered spiritual leaders, who agreed to give them an audience. He told them he had heard of three young boys who might possibly be the new incarnation, all living near Kumbum monastery. On investigating these leads, the search party found that the first child had already died and the second ran away crying when he saw them. The third lived in the remote village of Pari Takster.

A detachment from the group was sent to the village in disguise, with Lama Keutsang Rinpoche, who headed the search party, dressed as a servant, and a lesser official, Tsedrung Lobsang Tsewang, taking his place as leader. When they came across the house it exactly matched the vision in its appearance and position, with a peach tree blooming unseasonably early. They claimed to be pilgrims on their way to a Chinese shrine and asked for lodging. This was granted and, as protocol required, the family received the group leader whilst the 'servants' were taken to be fed. Playing in the kitchen was a small boy who, as soon as he saw the disguised Keutsang Rinpoche, shouted 'Lama! Lama!' This was particularly impressive since the family spoke the Amdo dialect in which the word for 'lama' was 'aga'. The child sat on the lama's lap and immediately grabbed the rosary he was wearing, saying,

'This is mine, please may I have it?' It was, indeed, the Thirteenth Dalai Lama's rosary. The lama told him he could have it if he guessed who he was, and the reply left him in no doubt that this was the reborn Dalai Lama.

'Sera-aga,' he replied.

Keutsang Rinpoche was, as stated, the leader of Sera, one of three great monasteries near Lhasa. The rest of the search party was called and more tests were carried out with the objects they had brought with them. The boy correctly identified everything that had belonged to the previous Dalai Lama. He was then given a physical examination which revealed further signs traditionally associated with their leader, who is said to be the divine incarnation of Chenrezi, the great Buddha of Mercy. These included a mark like a conch shell on his skin and two small bumps of flesh beneath the shoulder-blades which represent the two extra arms with which Chenrezi is often shown. Further evidence was provided by the two-year-old's ability to speak the Lhasa dialect which would have been familiar to him in his previous incarnation but would never have been spoken or heard in his home. He had, incidentally, often told his parents he was going to Lhasa one day.

It was the summer of 1935 when the boy, his family and the rest of the entourage made the long and difficult trek back to Tibet. On their arrival in Lhasa he provided further proof of his real identity, including a reference to a certain box which he said contained his teeth. When it was opened the Thirteenth Dalai Lama's false teeth were found inside.

THE RIVAL LAMAS

What makes the reincarnation of the Dalai Lama and other Tibetan Buddhist leaders unusual is that they appear to return in each lifetime to continue their work in the same role as they had in their previous life. For the rest of us, a new life brings new challenges and different responsibilities.

Just as the Panchen Lama played an important role in guiding the search party to the reborn Dalai Lama, so, too, the Dalai Lama is consulted after the death of the Panchen and other leading lamas. This can, however, present incredible problems for Tibet's spiritual leader, as recent history has shown.

After the death of the Tenth Panchen Lama in 1989 at the age of fifty-one, there was the usual search for his reincarnation – but by two rival search parties. On the one hand, Tibetan Buddhists generally were keen that their spiritual leader should be the first to identify the reborn Panchen. On the other, the Chinese authorities were keen that *they* should be responsible for finding and naming the new Panchen Lama. By doing so, they would not only stamp their authority on Tibet but would also be able to influence future events, since it would be their chosen Panchen who would, in time, be responsible for confirming the reincarnation of the next Dalai Lama when the present one dies.

In other words, rebirth was no longer only a spiritual or religious question. It had become a matter of international politics as well.

After a six-year search for the new Panchen Lama, the Dalai Lama publicly confirmed that six-year-old Gedhun Choekyi Nyima, the son of nomads, was the reincarnation they had been looking for.

However, the child and his parents have not been seen since the Dalai Lama's announcement was made and a request made to the Chinese authorities to let him be trained as a senior monk was rejected. They are thought to be under house arrest – probably in Beijing – and some fear for their lives. The abbot of Tashilhumpo monastery, Chadrel Rinpoche, also disappeared at about the same time, and was apparently taken into state custody. He had been the leader of the rival, official Chinese search party looking for the reincarnation, and it is clearly no coincidence that he was detained in Chengdu on 17 May 1995, just three days after the Dalai Lama identified Gedhun Choekyi Nyima as the reborn Panchen Lama. It seems likely – and the Chinese authorities clearly hold this view – that Chadrel Rinpoche and his search party had also identified the boy as the true reincarnation, and had somehow conveyed this information back to the Dalai Lama, whose own research had come to the same conclusion. By making his announcement, with some well-chosen words, the Tibetan leader-in-exile had stolen a march on China, leaving it with no alternative but to confirm his choice of Panchen Lama, or put forward its own candidate. It chose the latter course of action.

Seven months later, the Chinese named another six-year-old, Gyaincain Norbu, as their choice. Three possible candidates had been identified and interviewed at length by the official Chinese search party, guided by omens and other signs, but no single candidate was clearly the reincarnation. So the matter was decided by lottery – not unusual in Tibetan Buddhism – and the boys' names were inscribed on ivory markers and placed inside a golden urn. Under the watchful eye of Luo Gan, a senior Chinese official, and 200 or more Buddhist monks inside the Jokhang temple in Lhasa, Tibet, the urn was turned several times. The light of traditional yak-butter lamps flickered in the early dawn as a senior monk withdrew one of the markers. On it was the name Gyaincain Norbu, who was awaiting the outcome of the ceremony with the other two potential Panchens in a room at the temple.

A few days later, on 8 December 1995, Gyaincain Norbu's enthronement took place at Tashilhumpo monastery, the Panchen Lama's traditional home in the Tibetan city of Xigaze, attended by a member of China's cabinet, Li Tieying. The irony, of course, is that the Chinese government – the voice of communism which is officially atheist – was giving its full support and blessing to a Tibetan Buddhist reincarnation ceremony. There was clearly an ulterior motive.

The Panchen Lama crisis is not without precedent in Tibet, for there are also two Gyalwa Karmapas. As head of the 'Black Hats', the Kagyudpa sect of Tibetan Buddhism, founded in the eleventh century, the Karmapa is regarded as second only to the Dalai Lama, who is head of the 'Yellow Hats', the Gelugpa sect. The Karmapa's monastery is at Rumtek in Sikkim, once an independent kingdom in the Himalayas but now (since 1975) the twenty-second Indian state. Before his death he is always said to predict where, when and to whom he will be reborn. This should neatly overcome, one would expect, the problems that have manifested with the latest incarnation of the Panchen Lama and, if the proceedings were properly scrutinised, would even satisfy the demands of scientists for proof of reincarnation. But such hopes have been short-lived ...

THE 'DEMON LAMA'

The Gyalwa Karmapa's sixteenth incarnation came to an end in 1981. Knowing he was dying of cancer, he decided to take his final breath in America because 'my body is in the West and my mind will be born in the East.' He is said to have meant by this that he wanted to bless the whole hemisphere. His followers report that, during his final days, the cancer, diabetes and tuberculosis from which he suffered would all disappear suddenly, then reappear, from one day to the next, indicating that his was no ordinary body. The doctors in the Chicago hospital where he was treated are said to have been astonished when he died, because the area around his heart remained warm for a couple of days and his skin, rather than being cold, was still elastic. No medical records have been published to confirm these remarkable claims. And his rebirth as the Seventeenth Gyalwa Karmapa has been just as controversial. Following his normal practice, he did not make a verbal prediction about when, where and to whom he would be reborn. Instead, it was written down for all to read at a later date. But where did he put it? Usually, he would give it to a trusted individual with instructions to reveal its contents when the time was right. This time, he hid it.

For eight years his followers searched for the piece of paper that would herald his reincarnation. Then, his first disciple, Tai Situpa, remembered that the Karmapa had once given him a protective talisman (a box and cord), saying enigmatically, 'One day this will be useful.' On examining it more closely in 1990 Tai Situpa discovered the letter of prediction hidden inside. The Karmapa had written it in the form of a poem:

Emaho. Self-awareness is always bliss;
The dharmadhatu has no centre nor edge

From here to the north (in) the east of (the land) of snow
is a country where divine thunder spontaneously blazes

(In) a beautiful nomad's place with the sign of the cow,
the method is Dondrup and the wisdom is Logala
Born in the year of the one used for earth
(With) the miraculous, far-reaching sound of the white
    one:
(This) is the one known as Karmapa.

He is sustained by Lord Donyo Drupa.
Being non-sectarian, he pervades all directions;
Not staying close to some and distant from others, he is
    the protector of all beings:
The sun of the Buddha's Dharma, as benefits others,
    always blazes.

The Karmapa had four 'spiritual sons' who, on his death, acted as regents with responsibility for searching for his new incarnation. One of them, the Karmapa's blood relative, Kunzig Shamar – a nephew – immediately declared the letter a forgery and claimed that Tai Situpa, another regent, had written it. The Dalai Lama and the heads of all the other sects, however, authenticated the letter, not only by comparing it with the Karmapa's handwriting but also by using their psychic powers.

The decision was taken to send someone to Tibet in search of the reincarnated Karmapa, but the regent chosen, Jamgon Kong Frul, never reached his destination. He was killed in a mysterious car crash involving no other vehicle on an empty road. It seems his car hit a tree, but some Buddhists claim it showed signs of an explosion at the front. So, the search for the Seventeenth Karmapa now had to contend not only with allegations of fraud but with rumours of murder, too. The quest continued, however, and the written prediction proved remarkably accurate.

On 23 July 1992 the Dalai Lama's office announced that he

had granted his final seal of approval and recognition to the Seventeenth Gyalwa Karmapa who he named as Ugen Thinley alias Apo Gaga. Ugen Thinley was born on 26 June 1985 (wood-ox year) to Karma Dondrup Tashi and his wife Loga in the Bakor District, Lhathok Province, in occupied Tibet.

On this occasion, incidentally, the Chinese authorities were quick to recognise seven-year-old Ugen Thinley as the Seventeenth Karmapa. But regent Shamar Rinpoche – the man who alleged the letter was a fraud – was not. In February 1994 he smuggled his own candidate, ten-year-old Tenzin Chentse, out of Tibet, via Hong Kong, to the Indian capital, Delhi, and held a press conference to announce that *this* boy was the real Karmapa. Shamar admitted there was no prediction letter about his candidate but said the boy's birth was forecast in a message passed by the last Karmapa to an eminent lama of another sect who will be named 'at a suitable time'. It seems that time has not yet arrived, and meanwhile Ugen Thinley is undergoing his spiritual training at Tsurphu Monastery.

All this ought to be disconcerting, to say the least, for Tibetan Buddhists. But they seem to be able to accept such events stoically and with the same degree of tolerance and lack of aggression with which they have responded to the Chinese rape of their land and people. A non-Tibetan expert on Buddhism sheds some light on this. Canadian-born Norma Levine, who has Jewish origins, told the story of the power struggle in *Reincarnation International Magazine*, No 2:

> The curious thing is there were a series of predictions by the Karmapa more than 500 years ago in which he said that between the sixteenth and seventeenth incarnations the lineage would almost die out. There would be reborn a demon lama and he even called him Natha, which means relative or nephew. The Karmapa said that through the power of his twisted aspirations the lineage of the Karmapas would nearly be destroyed.

She is certain it will not be, however, because the coming of the Karmapa – which means 'master of activity' – was predicted by the Buddha who said he would have twenty-one incarnations. So, it seems that good will triumph over evil, and the Seventeenth Karmapa will live to die four more times.

Similarly, world politics should not be capable of preventing the true Dalai Lama and Panchen Lama continuing on their soul journeys and being reborn time and again to look after their people's spiritual needs.

Perhaps it is time for science to take a closer look at the methods and results of the Tibetan reincarnation search parties to provide independent verification of the events surrounding each identification. Maybe Tibetan Buddhism will one day extend an invitation to researchers to participate in such searches – not to play a role in the final decision-making process but to ensure that the procedures employed satisfy scientific demands.

Imagine the impact if the next rebirth of the Dalai Lama had not only the Panchen Lama's seal of approval but that of a leading global scientific institution as well.

chapter nine

NO WAY TO BEHAVE

THE GIRL WHO DROWNED AND CAME BACK

*T*eenage rebellion is a well-known social phenomenon in most societies, but in children who remember past lives a refusal to conform can occur a lot earlier – sometimes when they can barely speak. Imagine, for example, the distress Dilukshi caused when, at the age of two, she refused to call her parents 'mother' and 'father'. Instead, she insisted on addressing her mother as 'clooche' which means aunt in Sri Lanka. Then, to add insult to injury, she demanded to be taken to her 'real' home in Dambulla, which was over 62 miles (100 kilometres) away. Much as they loved their little daughter, her parents reacted as most of us would in the circumstances by trying to reason with her and dispel her fantasy.

Dilukshi, however, was adamant. In fact, she even chided her mother and father for the way they treated her. Her 'real' parent, she explained, *never* shouted at her. Instead, they called her 'darling' or 'sweet little daughter'. She went on to explain that she had once drowned in a river near Dambulla. Troubled by their daughter's persistent statements about a past life, they decided that the high priest of the Dambulla temple might be able to help – which he did, in a rather unconventional way. He passed the problem to a feature writer, I.W. Abeypala, on *Weekend* newspaper who gave the story maximum publicity. In fact, this was not as irresponsible as it may sound. It meant that there was a written and published record of Dilukshi's statements about her former life before any attempt was made to corroborate them.

One of the story's readers was a man who thought Dilukshi's account of her life and death sounded very similar to that of his daughter Shiromi who had died in September 1983, one year before Dilukshi was born. He and his wife contacted the newspaper and the journalist arranged for the child and her parents to visit Dambulla for a meeting. On their arrival, Dilukshi led the way confidently, as I.W. Abeypala reported to his readers: 'I was there and saw the child herself identify the parents of her previous birth. She recognised her parents, the brother, sister, her aunt, her grandmother. I saw with my own eyes how she recognised them, so I accept that as proof.'

Dilukshi also identified various belongings of Shiromi, including a drawing book with a half-completed picture which she promptly finished. However, as Professor Erlendur Haraldsson pointed out later, when he investigated the case, since no attempt was made to mix these with items which did *not* belong to Shiromi, there was no scientific value to this test. Dilukshi then led the group to the river bank and pointed to the exact spot where she, as nine-year-old Shiromi, had fallen in. Before being taken to Dambulla she had described the place, saying that there was a footbridge nearby and that the spot was also close to her father's paddy-fields. There was no footbridge when the group arrived, but one *did* exist at the time Shiromi fell into the river and drowned.

The story of Shiromi's rebirth as Dilukshi was featured in Jeffrey Iverson's excellent BBC TV documentary *In Search of the Dead*, on which his book of the same name was based. He testified:

> It was clear Shiromi's parents accept Dilukshi as their daughter returned. We took the child and her parents there, to film the two families together, and they made a party of it. Dilukshi was totally at home and brought small presents for the younger brother and sister of her previous life. It was a reunion that was somehow both happy and sad.

In looking for corroboration of such cases, we tend to place most emphasis on checking the statements made by a child against the facts we are able to verify. But we should not over-look the remarkable behaviour of children remembering past lives. Sometimes their memories are not very precise. Maybe they cannot remember names or details very accurately. But they often exhibit traits, strength of character and determination that are clearly not the product of their present life because they are too young to have been influenced in such a way and they are often in conflict with their parents' views.

In Dilukshi's case, here was a child who could barely speak, refusing in a very positive and direct way to call her parents 'mother' and 'father' because she still identified very strongly with another mother and father.

THE TEA-PICKERS' DAUGHTER

It was the way Subashini drank tea which baffled her quite prosperous parents in Sri Lanka. She would put a little sugar in the palm of her hand and lick it as she drank the tea. She did this not in an experimental way but as though it were a custom. Yet neither her parents, nor anyone they knew, drank tea that way, so she was certainly not copying others.

They were equally puzzled by her inordinate fear of tropical thunderstorms until, during one of these at the age of three, she told them she had died in her previous life when torrential rain had caused a huge landslide to bury the house in which she lived.

Subashini was also able to describe tea bushes – which were not grown in the part of the island where she now lived – and demonstrate how tea-pickers worked. Her parents learned from her that she had been the daughter of tea-pickers who had worked on a plantation at Sinhapitiya, Gampola, some 62 miles (100 kilometres) away. She also spoke of Tamil workers but said her own family, in that life, were Sinhalese Buddhists. Subashini was able to describe in detail events surrounding a great storm which brought down part of the mountain which towered over the plantation and killed her and other members of her family. Following her mother's instructions, she recalled, 'I took a torch and went outside and came here.' She knew, however, that an elder brother had escaped because he had returned home and then gone out again.

One day, when her father was invited to a wedding close to where Subashini had indicated she had lived, he decided to take her with him. As they approached the plantation, however, she became so scared of being trapped that he had to turn back before speaking to any members of families affected by the disaster. But it was not difficult for researchers Godwin Samararatne and Tissa Jayawardane to check the accuracy of the child's story when they learned of her memories shortly afterwards. They discovered that, exactly as she had said, a disaster had struck the area in October 1977, just over two years before she was born, when twenty-eight people lost their lives. A storm had caused a landslide which had buried many of the tea-pickers' homes, including that of the only Sinhalese Buddhist family. The mother, father and three children – including a girl of seven, Devi Mallika – perished. An older brother had been in the house earlier, just as Subashini had said, but had left before the landslide. An elder sister was not at home that night. Of the thirty-two statements made by the infant Subashini, twenty-five were found to be true.

The surviving brother and sister still work on the plantation and were able to explain Subashini's strange tea-drinking habits. Their family had been poor, they revealed, and could not afford to buy enough sugar to put into a cup. Instead, they put sugar in the palm of their hand and licked it between sips of tea – just as the reborn Devi Mallika appears to have done in the body of Subashini.

THE CHILD SHOPKEEPER

Because of its caste system, India is the country in which behavioural differences are likely to be most startling if an individual is reborn outside his or her family or culture. It is probably for this reason that so many striking cases of children 'behaving badly' or just differently come from India.

In the case of Parmod Sharma, second son of Professor Bankeybehary Lal Sharma, a Sanskrit scholar and professor at an intermediate college in Bisauli, Uttar Pradesh, one of the first signs that he had past-life memories was when he told his mother not to cook because he had a wife in Moradabad who could prepare their food. Parmod Sharma, born on 11 October 1944, was then about two-and-a-half years old! He then complained about his family's financial status which compared unfavourably with his previous, prosperous life. He went on to explain that he was one of the 'Moran Brothers' and he had a large soda and biscuit shop in Moradabad, and another shop in Saharanpur. He had become ill in that life, he explained, after eating too much curd cheese and had died in the bath. In this life, incidentally, he did not like curd cheese and had a fear of being submerged in water. Parmod Sharma spent much of his childhood building model shops and making mud cakes. Word of his behaviour reached the family of Parmanand Mehra, whose life he appeared to be remembering, in Moradabad.

When the two families met, Parmod Sharma insisted that his sons from his previous life called him 'father', even though they were, of course, older than him. 'I have only become small,' he explained to them. He recognised several people and places – among them his wife 'with whom I always quarrelled' – and also identified people he had known in his previous life when he was taken to Saharanpur. As well as many other statements which were confirmed he said that he (as Parmanand Mehra) had read his sister-in-law's palm. This interest in palmistry had carried over into his present life.

Meeting his past-life family had a strong emotional impact on Parmod Sharma. He was very reluctant to leave Moradabad after his first visit and wept when taken away from the Mehra family. Shortly afterwards he disappeared from home and was found at Bisauli railway station, intent on getting a train to Saharanpur 'to run the family business there.'

THE YOUNG LOTHARIO

From the moment he began to speak, Bishen Chand talked about his past life as Laxmi Barain, the only son of a wealthy landowner who not only spoilt him and gave him a taste for luxury and extravagance but also obligingly died when the boy was in his late teens, leaving him a substantial inheritance to squander. The story that emerged from the child's lips was startling enough and it didn't help that he criticised his father for his present life's poverty, demanded money and cried when he did not receive it. He also made many disparaging remarks about the family and the circumstances into which he had been born.

'Even my servant would not take the food cooked here,' he shouted. And when given cotton clothes he tore them off, demanding silk ones. He would not give the clothes worn by his family to his servants, he said with disdain. Of course, he had no servants in this life, but Laxmi Barain certainly did. In fact, on one occasion, seeing a man coming from the apartment of a prostitute, Padma, with whom he believed he had an exclusive arrangement, he took his servant's gun and shot the man dead. It seems likely that his wealth was sufficient to bribe the authorities and he was never sentenced for the crime. But, as Bishen Chand, he freely confessed to it. He also admitted that he had spent his substantial inheritance on good food, fine clothes, beautiful women and alcohol.

With such a past-life it is, perhaps, not surprising to learn that at five-and-a-half he asked his father, 'Papa, why don't you keep a mistress? You will have great pleasure from her.' When asked what pleasure, Bishen Chand replied, 'You will enjoy the fragrance of her hair and feel much joy from her company.'

Bishen and Padma the prostitute met in 1944 when he was twenty-three and she was fifty-two. 'Are you Padma?' he asked. 'Yes,' she replied. He then embraced her ... and fainted. Later that day, fully recovered, he set off with a bottle of wine, intent on renewing the friendship that they had both enjoyed when he was Laxmi Barain. But Padma would not hear of it. 'I am an old woman like your mother,' she reproached him. 'You lost everything in your previous life. Now you want to lose everything again.' And with that she smashed the bottle of wine.

Surprisingly, although Bishen Chand spoke about his past life daily when he was a child, neither his parents nor his brothers and sisters scolded him for his criticisms or tried to repress his memories.

THE BRAHMIN REBORN INTO A LOWER CASTE

In an even earlier case, that of Jagdish Chandra, the child began asking his father to get a car almost as soon as he could talk. He insisted on eating first, before other members of the family, refused to eat with non-Hindus or to have food prepared by them, and was very hostile towards men with beards.

His father, K.K.N. Sahay, a lawyer, at first made light of his son's request for him to get a car but eventually asked his young son where he should get it from. Jagdish Chandra replied that he should get *his* car, which was at the home of his father, Babuji, in Benares. Appreciating the value of written evidence, Jagdish Chandra's father made a careful note of all his son's statements, then wrote a letter to an English language newspaper, the *Leader*, asking for help in checking the existence of a man named Babuji Pandey living in the city of Benares, an important place of pilgrimage on the river Ganges, whose son Jai Gopal had died.

It did not take long before confirmation came from several sources who were also able to verify at least twenty-four of the thirty-six statements made by Jagdish Chandra and recorded in writing. They also threw light on his strange behaviour even before the two families met. Jagdish Chandra's memories, incidentally, were not vague generalisations, but very specific. For example, he said that his (Jai Gopal's) father drank *bhang*, an intoxicating drink made from Indian hemp, 'paints his face with powder or earth before his bath on washing his face in the morning', and was a *panda* – a supervisor of a bathing pier by the river who assisted pilgrims who went to bathe there. He also said his father listened to the songs of a prostitute named Bhagwati and that he had had a brother, Jai Mangal, who died of poisoning. All these claims were shown to be correct.

Babu Pandey and his family were Brahmins, whereas Jagdish Chandra's family belonged to the Kayastha caste. This would explain the reborn child's insistence on eating first: it was usual for Brahmins to be asked to take the first food if they were eating with people of other castes and young Jagdish Chandra still clearly regarded himself as a Brahmin. His dislike of bearded men can also be attributed to Brahmins' well-known dislike of Muslims.

His love of cars was another matter. This definitely seemed to stem from Babu Pandey's indulgence of Jai Gopal who was taken for daily drives around Benares. 'It seems Jai Gopal was rather pampered,' Professor Stevenson observed, and in his new life this appears to have continued, for K.K.N. Sahay also purchased several cars, one after the other, apparently to keep his young son happy.

Even if Jagdish Chandra had somehow acquired the information he gave normally, 'we should still have to account in this case, as in so many others, for the strong behavioural traits related to the previous life,' writes Stevenson. 'No Kayastha parent would consider for a minute drilling (or allowing anyone else to drill) his child in the habits and manners of Brahmins. Such an idea seems quite preposterous ...'

Jagdish Chandra made fifty-one statements in all, of which thirty-six were recorded in writing before verification was attempted; of these, at least twenty-four were confirmed before the two families met. He continued to visit his past-life family after those first encounters and they became very fond of him.

Unusually, Jagdish Chandra's memories seem to have persisted into adulthood. He went to Lucknow University, trained as a lawyer, and practises law today in his native city of Bareilly, still able to testify to his previous-life memories to those who show an interest.

THE UNTOUCHABLE REBORN AS A BRAHMIN

Most of the cases examined so far in this chapter have concerned individuals who appear to have been 'demoted' from one life to the next. In other words, they seem to have been reborn into a life without the material advantages – cars, servants, fine clothes, large houses – to which they had become accustomed, even if for only a few years. And, not surprisingly, they complain. There are other cases, however, where the person returns in far better circumstances but that, as we shall see, can cause just as many problems.

In the case of Swaran Lata, for example, her rebirth into a Brahmin family was most certainly a 'promotion' since the previous life she remembered was that of an untouchable – a member of the lowest caste. Unfortunately, she brought with her from that life coarse manners and personal habits which did not go down well with her new family. Lovable though she was, they regarded her behaviour as repulsively dirty. Unlike the other family members, for example, she willingly cleaned up the excrement of younger children; in fact she seemed eager to do it. And she horrified her vegetarian family by asking for pork.

THE GIRL WITH TWO FAMILIES

Such reports also challenge our own perceptions of what makes a 'good' life. In the case of Manju Sharma, investigated by Dr Satwant Pasricha in India, for example, we also have a child born to a Brahmin family who could remember a much poorer life, when she belonged to the tradesmen's caste. At the age of two-and-a-half, Manju began talking of the life she led in Chaumuha village as Krishna Devi, which came to an abrupt end at the age of ten when she fell into a well. These memories came to light when she recognised an uncle, Tanji, from that life and spoke to him about her memories. He arranged for her previous-life mother to visit her and she was very loving. Recalling those early events in her present life, she told author Jeffrey Iverson: 'Then my brother from the village took me to my parents' house. I stayed there for ten years.'

Having lived half of this life with her 'real' parents and the other with her past-life parents does not seem to have caused Manju Sharma any emotional or psychological problems. She is now married with two children of her own and continues to visit Krishna Devi's family. It is clear from her testimony that the material advantages of her new life as a Brahmin held little attraction for Manju Sharma, who much preferred the humble

surroundings full of love provided by the parents she remembered so well from her last life. They, too, made it clear that they did not regard her as Manju. 'She is Krishna,' her past-life father insisted. 'She is Krishna, she is our daughter Krishna of her previous life. We wait for her to come home.' He also treated her daughters as if they were his own grandchildren, explaining: 'They are not outsiders – they are my very own.'

chapter ten

SPECIAL TALENTS

Why were Mozart, Schubert and Mendelssohn – to name only three famous child prodigies – born with the ability to make beautiful music? All three had begun composing before they reached the age of twelve. And Johann Hummel, Chopin and Yehudi Menuhin were so musically gifted that they were giving concerts at the age of eleven. At the same age, Pascal was deprived of mathematical books by his father, yet he secretly devised a geometry of his own. Meanwhile, the eighteenth-century German prodigy Christian Heinecken was speaking Latin and German by the age of three, as well as giving public demonstrations of his knowledge of history, geography and Bible study. Sadly, his potential was never realised because he died a year later.

Music, in particular, seems to inspire infant geniuses, but there have been child prodigies in many other disciplines. Their talents are so awe-inspiring that some people have suggested that they may even have brought their abilities with them from a past life. It has to be said, however, that child prodigies themselves make no such claims and in some respects the suggestion seems to cast doubt on the genuineness of their talent and the efforts they put into their achievements. Nevertheless, there is a very good case for looking at special skills or aptitudes in people claiming to remember past lives to see if they add to the evidence for reincarnation.

LORD BURLINGTON'S SISTER

Take, for example, the case of Lyndi Clement, a London mother of four, who still has strong memories of a life she lived in Georgian times. In fact, from her earliest childhood days she can remember feeling as if she were not living in the right period, that she 'didn't fit in'. Often, as she is driven along twentieth-century roads, the images through the windows change and she experiences her surroundings as they were 200 years ago. 'I hear the noises – dogs barking, horses' hooves clattering, people shouting,' she told author Sue Carpenter, who reported the case in *Past Lives: True Stories of Reincarnation*. 'I see beggars walking around and smell different odours. I've never questioned it; it has always been part of my life.'

Soon after the book was published I was asked by a TV company to bring together a group of people prepared to discuss their experiences and Lyndi Clement was one of those who accepted the invitation. She believes she was Elizabeth Boyle, the sister of Lord Burlington, in her past life – a fact that emerged during hypnotic regression. Her strong identification with the Georgian period has given her an advantage over others in her profession. She is a wardrobe mistress with Opera Restor'd, has been researching a major exhibition on pleasure gardens for the past four years, and also organises the decorating and furnishing of country houses before they are opened to the public – all work in which she draws on her past-life memories to ensure that the details are correct. Her fascination with the domestic side of the period led her to attend the Royal School of Needlework and she now teaches needlework and eighteenth-century dress design, corset-making and pattern-cutting as well.

THE RAF RADIO OPERATOR

Another first-class example of a special talent being carried over into this life was presented to me by a young Englishman living in Holland. Martin Heald agreed to let *Reincarnation International* have an exclusive on his story and later co-operated with me and a TV company in making it into an exciting documentary. Martin Heald believes he was an RAF radio operator shot down during the Second World War – and he has been able to produce some impressive evidence.

His past-life memories began as a child and were triggered

by the discovery of an old telephone handset in his parents' wardrobe. His father was explaining how it was used to send Morse code messages by tapping out long or short signals and he demonstrated this by sending the international emergency signal – SOS. Instantly the scene changed and Martin saw and heard the sounds of an aircraft after it had been hit. These same scenes appeared later in his life, particularly while he was watching television programmes on the fiftieth anniversary of VE day, and so he decided to investigate them further. He was now living outside Amsterdam with his girlfriend and he consulted a hypnotherapist who was able to take him back to the life he appeared to have lived. Now he was able to describe the attack on the aircraft in greater detail and he knew, when it exploded, that his body would never be found. Martin Heald was able to give his past-life name, Richard Seymour, and various other details of his life, including the fact that his father had been a clergyman. In time, he was able to verify these details through war records which showed that Richard Seymour was a radio operator whose aircraft had been shot down over the North Sea, exactly as he had described. The crew all died and Seymour's body was never recovered.

What has this to do with special talents? In this life, Martin Heald decided to join the Royal Air Force (before he had any understanding of what those childhood 'flashbacks' meant) and underwent various tests. When he returned for his results he was asked whether he had ever learned Morse code. He said he had not. 'Well,' he was told, 'you scored 100 per cent. That's the first time that has happened in the history of the RAF.' There were no vacancies for the job he really wanted; instead he accepted a job as a radio operator. It was only years later, after he had been regressed, that he realised the significance of the work he did in relation to his past-life.

INHERITED SKILLS

Like the Brazilian boy Paulo Lorenz (mentioned in Chapter Four), who claimed to be the reincarnation of his dead sister Emilia, and also possessed her great sewing skills, Corliss Chotkin, a North American Tlingit Indian, said to have been his uncle, Victor Vincent, in a previous life, displayed a similar love of boats and being on water. He taught himself how to run boat engines without any lessons and even repaired a broken engine which his father could not mend. Imad Elawar, a Lebanese boy who appears to have been the reincarnation of French-speaking Ibrahim Bouhamzy, proved to be a very fast learner of the French language at school. Both these cases will be dealt with in greater depth in later chapters.

Disna Samarasinghe showed unusual piety and also a precocious knowledge of household chores, such as cooking and thatch weaving, which corresponded with traits in the person she claimed to have been in her former life. Similarly, Lalitha Abeyawardena, when she was a young child, played at being a teacher and, like Disna, showed an unusual interest in religious practices. Nilanthie, the woman whose life she claimed to remember, had been a schoolteacher and a person of renowned piety.

Not all inherited traits are good. There have been cases of children who remembered lives as thieves and who used those skills in their current lives to pick pockets and commit other larcenies.

Professor Ian Stevenson argues that, since there is evidence for reincarnation, we should consider it as a contributing factor in the process which makes each of us unique. In other words, it may not be just 'the chance shuffling of genes' which makes us the way we are. Which brings us back to the question: What inspires child prodigies?

'Many children show early in life an interest in the work they later take up as adults,' Professor Stevenson observes in *Children Who Remember Previous Lives*.

Among great musicians one can find numerous examples of parental influences that seem to explain adequately the early expression of interest and skill in music. For example, the fathers of Bach, Mozart, Beethoven, Brahms, and Elgar were all musicians. But Dvořák's father was a butcher, Delius's a businessman, Mendelssohn's a banker (albeit a cultured one), and

Handel's a barber-surgeon. The case of Handel seems particularly instructive. His father opposed Handel's interest in music, which he showed in early childhood. His mother gave him no effective support, and although an aunt encouraged him, her influence seems insufficient to have counteracted by itself the stern opposition of Handel's father. The family had no known ancestors with an interest in music.

Though there is no evidence that Handel or his family believed him to be the reincarnation of a talented composer, Professor Stevenson is arguing that any attempt to understand how Handel – and other gifted people – had such a gift from childhood should consider rebirth memories as well as genetic explanations.

DO CHILDREN'S GAMES MIRROR THEIR PAST LIVES?

If he had not remembered and spoken about his past life as a shopkeeper, the parents of Wijanama Kithsiri might have wondered why, when he came home from school, he always liked to play shops. In the same way, their previous-life memories seem to explain why Ma Tin Aung Myo and Bajrang B. Saxena played soldiers; why Vias Rajpal took his playmates' temperatures and listened to their chests; and why Daniel Jirdi crawled under the sofa and made believe he was mending a car.

More disturbingly, some children have been known to dramatise their problems or even the cause of their death in a previous life. There are case studies, for example, of two children who remembered being alcoholics in their former incarnation and imitated drunks staggering around and then collapsing. Ramez Sharns enacted shooting himself, having committed suicide this way in his past life. Maung Win Aung liked to play with a rope around his neck. He, needless to say, could remember a suicidal death by hanging.

There is strong evidence, then, that some people not only bring past-life memories into this life but also behavioural patterns and aptitudes. But is it reasonable to assume, when a talent appears at an unexpectedly early age in a child, that it has been carried over from another life? Could there be other explanations?

'ARTIFICIAL REINCARNATION'

Any attempt to answer this question has to take into account the remarkable experiments of a Russian parapsychologist who coined the phrase 'artificial reincarnation'. Dr Vladimir L. Raikov's research is very different to that of investigators like Professor Stevenson who look for naturally occurring past-life recall. In truth, Dr Raikov is not remotely concerned with the concept of living many lives. Instead, he concentrates on the mind's tremendous potential which is largely untapped by the majority of humans.

Raikov discovered in the 1960s a powerful hypnotic technique which, he claimed, induced 'a new form of active trance'. In this altered state of consciousness, which he described as an exceedingly deep trance, the subject was told that he or she was someone famous with special talents. The individual was then asked to demonstrate the abilities possessed by that person and, remarkably, over a very short space of time, they developed the same skills.

Reporting on these experiments, A. Tsipko told readers of *Komsomolskaya Pravda* (12 November 1966) about a demonstration he had witnessed in a large, sunlit studio in Moscow. A group of art students were drawing a model from life when Raikov arrived with the writer.

'I want you to meet one of my best students,' he said as he motioned towards a young woman in her early twenties. Ira stood up, turned to the visitor, extended a hand and said, 'I am Raphael of Urbino.' When asked what year it was she replied, 'Why, 1505, of course.'

Writing about this meeting in their book *Psychic Discoveries Behind the Iron Curtain*, Sheila Ostrander and Lynn Schroeder explain that psychiatrist Raikov had no need to go in search of corroboration of what she was saying because he knew 'how this Raphael became reincarnated' just as he knew 'how the other three Raphaels in the class came into the flesh again. Raikov called them into being. He is a master hypnotist.'

Raikov, therefore, was not exploring rebirth but endeavouring 'to evoke the birth of talent'. He seems to have been outstandingly successful in many cases. Alla, a high-ranking physics student at Moscow University, was told that she was Ilya Repin, the great Russian painter. 'You think like Repin. You *see* like Repin. You have the abilities of Repin. You *are* Repin,' Raikov coaxed. 'Consequently, the talent of Repin is yours to command.'

Before this experiment, Alla had neither interest nor talent in drawing, as she readily demonstrated to Raikov and his team. Yet, after a few 'reincarnation' sessions, she was drawing much better.

'She began, after ten afternoons as Repin, to want to draw in her own time and took to carrying a sketch pad,' Ostrander and Schroeder continue:

> In three months, when Raikov brought her to the end of her 25-lesson course, Alla drew like a professional – not like Repin or Raphael, two of her many reincarnations, but as well as a competent magazine illustrator. Her new talent exploded so vibrantly in Alla that she's seriously considering chucking her physics theorems and letting loose at the easel full time.

This result was by no means unique. When Raikov and his collaborators ran their initial tests with twenty young unartistic but intelligent students, each of whom was told he was a genius of some kind, 'everyone wound up, in his opinion, with a newfound talent'. The results were often so stunning that the students themselves, when they returned to their normal selves, refused to believe that they had created the pictures they were shown.

There is no suggestion, it seems, that by 'becoming' a famous artist the subject can paint in his style. What happens is that the act of believing that they are someone with a special gift enhances the subjects' confidence and concentration, and destroys their inhibitions and creative blocks. After a time their newly acquired facility becomes second nature.

I know of no similar studies being carried out in the West to replicate Raikov's work and, as I have already said, it has no direct bearing on the case for reincarnation. However, it does appear to demonstrate the tremendous creativity of the mind and how cautious we need to be in drawing conclusions about some manifestations of past-life memories.

chapter eleven

IN TWO MINDS

BRIDEY MURPHY

Until the 1950s, very few people claimed to remember a past life, and those who did were mostly to be found in countries such as India, Thailand, Burma and Sri Lanka. But all that was to change with the publication of an American book which seemed to reveal a way in which we could all recall previous incarnations. Morey Bernstein's *The Search for Bridey Murphy* told of his hypnotic experiments with Virginia Burns Tighe whose real identity he hid behind the pseudonym of Ruth Mills Simmons. Under hypnosis she claimed to be Bridey Murphy, the daughter of a barrister, Duncan Murphy, born in County Cork, Republic of Ireland, on 20 December 1798.

During six tape-recorded sessions between November 1952 and October 1953 the hypnotised subject said she lived at 'The Meadows' outside Cork, had a brother, Duncan, who was two years older, and a younger brother who had died as a baby of 'black something'. As the sessions progressed, the Colorado housewife's voice took on a stronger Irish brogue and her speech became more personalised. She told Bernstein that she had gone to a day school during the week which was run by a Mrs Strayne and had been there until around the age of fifteen. Her brother Duncan had, in fact, married Mrs Strayne's daughter Aimee.

The fascinating story caught the public imagination, became an international bestseller for the Pueblo, Colorado business-man-turned-hypnotist, and was even made into a movie. It also inspired many other amateur and professional hypnotists to conduct similar experiments and suddenly, it seemed, everyone could explore their past lives.

The story which emerged under hypnosis was remarkably detailed and contained many unlikely statements which seemed to indicate that fantasy or imagination alone were not responsible. Although a Protestant, said Tighe under hypnosis, Bridey married a Roman Catholic, Sean Brian Joseph MacCarthy, and there were two ceremonies: one in Cork, the other in Belfast. She even named the priest who married them in Northern Ireland – Father John Joseph Goran – and gave the name and location of his church: St Theresa's Church, Belfast. 'Bridey' also used Irish words which Bernstein did not understand and explained what they meant when asked. For example, she spoke of 'brates' (a little wishing cup) and 'lough' (a river or lake). The latter is now used only in relation to lakes. In fact, in those six sessions a wealth of verifiable factual and cultural evidence poured out. She was even able to dance a jig.

But was this really a past-life memory released by hypnosis? Or was it just a fantasy, cryptomnesia (the ability of the subconscious to remember things which the conscious mind no longer recalls), or even fraud? Bernstein himself had not been able to go to Ireland to check on the details but his publishers arranged for an Irish legal firm, librarians and others to conduct investigations. They found much that was accurate in Bridey Murphy's account but also encountered a major stumbling block; records of births, deaths and marriages did not exist in Ireland until 1864 – the year Bridey Murphy died.

The American newspapers of the day turned the Bridey Murphy story into a battleground. The *Chicago Daily News* serialised it and the *Chicago American* 'exposed' it, claiming that Tighe lived opposite an Irish aunt named Bridey Corkell (*née* Murphy) who could have told her stories about life in Ireland as a child. It was true that Tighe *did* have an aunt, but she had a different name and they had not met until she was eighteen. The aunt's name was Mrs Marie Burns and she was born in New York, not Ireland, was of Scottish-Irish descent and had spent most of her life in Chicago.

Because of this controversy there are some books on reincarnation which dismiss the Bridey Murphy story as either fraud or cryptomnesia. But it has many defenders, too, among them *Denver Post* journalist William J. Barker who spent three weeks in Ireland researching the story. His findings were published in a 19,000-word report, *The Truth About Bridey Murphy*, which appeared as a special twelve-page supplement to his newspaper on 11 March 1956 and was widely reprinted in other US and Canadian dailies.

In later editions of Bernstein's book, including the paperback, the publishers have added two chapters by Barker in which he details the evidence he uncovered and expresses his opinion of the many newspapers which have since chosen to ignore it, replacing facts with uninformed opinions by so-called experts:

> Prime offenders on this score were a national picture weekly … a Chicago newspaper, and certain of the ecclesiastical press. A Canadian magazine, for instance, printed a sizeable picture of Bernstein captioned, 'Hypnotist Morey Bernstein hoaxed the world with search for Bridey Murphy.' The accompanying text added in part, 'Only after he'd written a bestseller did Bernstein shamefacedly admit that *The Search for Bridey Murphy* belonged on the fiction, not the non-fiction shelves.' And a Chicago newspaper boldly claimed to have 'exposed the Denver Bridey Murphy and she admitted her story was a hoax.' Both statements, of course, were simply not in any wise the truth, and were termed libellous by Morey's attorneys.

One of the best summaries of the evidence for and against Bridey Murphy being a real past-life memory of Virginia Burns Tighe was written by C.J. Ducasse, Professor Emeritus of Philosophy at America's Brown University, Providence, Rhode Island, and published in the *Journal* of the American Society for Psychical Research in January 1962. It also appears as a chapter, 'Bridey Murphy Revisited', in *Reincarnation in the Twentieth Century*, edited by Martin Ebon. In this, Professor Ducasse refutes most of the allegations made against the hypnotist and his subject but says the evidence is not strong as far as reincarnation is concerned. It does, on the other hand, 'constitute fairly strong evidence that, in hypnotic trances, *paranormal* knowledge of one or another of several possible kinds concerning those recondite facts on nineteenth-century Ireland, became manifest'.

This is a view with which Professor Ian Stevenson would probably agree. An outspoken critic of much that goes on under the name of past-life regression, Stevenson has nevertheless corrected critics on a number of occasions when they have dismissed the Bridey Murphy case as a fabrication.

Bernstein, incidentally, was certainly not the first person to try such experiments. He is said to have carried out his research after reading a book by an English psychiatrist, Alexander Cannon, who claimed to have regressed more than 1,300 subjects. A French psychic investigator, Colonel Albert de Rochas, was conducting similar research in his Paris home around the turn of the century, regressing subjects through a whole series of past lives. But little of what he did was backed up by evidence and he did not believe his experiments proved the existence of reincarnation.

THE BLOXHAM TAPES

In the forty or more years since the Bernstein book opened people's minds to past-life hypnotic regression, there has been an explosion of public interest in the subject and countless other books recording similar stories, but few with the same impact. An exception is *More Lives Than One* by Jeffrey Iverson, published in 1976, based on tape-recordings of 400 regressions conducted by a talented hypnotist, Arnall Bloxham, who had been carrying out past-life research since 1940 at his Cardiff, South Wales, home. A careful and respected researcher, Bloxham was elected president of the British Society of Hypnotherapists in 1972.

Many of his regression subjects had consulted him, in the first place, with problems which they hoped would respond to hypnotherapy and then agreed to co-operate with his research.

One of these, Jane Evans, had no interest in reincarnation when she consulted Bloxham about rheumatism. She recalled seven lives under hypnosis, including one as a young Jewish mother, Rebecca, in twelfth-century York which ended with the massacre of Jews in that city in 1190. She recalled that, as a Jew, she had to wear a badge to signify her religion, and she also spoke of the money-lending trades common among the Jews in York and Lincoln. At first, it seemed as if the badge-wearing was a mistake, for it was not until 1215 that the Church authorities in Rome decreed that Jews in Christian countries must wear these insignia. But Iverson's research showed that it was already widespread in England in the twelfth century, before the proclamation.

Another aspect of her remarkably detailed story was also thought to be wrong at the time. Speaking of the terrible massacre, in which some Jews killed their own families rather than let them die at the hands of Gentiles, Jane Evans recalled how she and her children had gone into hiding in the crypt of a church in the hope of escaping death. But they were found and murdered. The problem with this story was that the churches in York were not designed with crypts.

Among those consulted by Jeffrey Iverson in researching his book was Professor Barrie Dobson, an authority on Jewish history at York University, who listened to the tape-recordings of Rebecca's past-life recollections and was impressed by their accuracy. Some of the facts, he felt sure, would be known only to professional historians. He also pointed out that, although some of the detail was technically wrong, it was what the Jews at that time believed to have happened. According to Iverson, Dobson was even able to identify the church into which she had fled as St Mary's in Castlegate.

Then, six months after he had given his verdict, Dobson contacted Iverson with some exciting news about St Mary's. 'During the renovation of the church, a workman found something that seemed to have been a crypt – very rare in York … It was blocked up immediately and before the York archaeologists could investigate it properly.' But, from the workman's description, it appeared to be either Norman or Romanesque, which predated the 1190 massacre. Having analysed the case in depth, and after pointing out that her account under hypnosis often ignored the best-known historical facts of life in twelfth-century York, Iverson concluded that her memories appeared to be 'not a straightforward reworking of history book versions of the massacre'.

In another of her lives, Jane Evans recalled living in medieval France about 1450 as a young Egyptian servant named Alison in the household of Jacques Coeur, the outstanding merchant prince of that period. She was able to describe in great detail his intrigues and talk about Agnes Sorel, the King's mistress, as well as Coeur's fall from favour after Agnes Sorel's death. She knew he had been arrested but knew nothing more than that because he had given her a poisoned draught which she took, ending her life.

DOUBT CAST ON REBECCA AND ALISON

But according to Melvin Harris, a sceptic who has been described as 'a great detective of the supernatural', the Jane Evans regressions do not provide any evidence for reincarnation. In his book, *Sorry You've Been Duped!*, Harris dismisses the 'Rebecca' memories as 'clearly a fantasy ... an amalgamation of at least two different stories of persecution taken from widely separated centuries'. He points out that on four occasions during the regressions Rebecca spoke of the Jewish community in York being forced to wear yellow badges which she describes as 'circles over our hearts'. He maintains that the Jewish badge was not introduced until the next century and the English pattern was two oblong white strips of cloth, representing the tablets of Moses; not the yellow circle, which was the badge worn in France and Germany after 1215. As for the crypt in which Rebecca and her children are said to have hidden, Harris is equally dismissive and is backed by Professor Barrie Dobson who had appeared to be a supporter of the crypt story in Iverson's book.

Professor Dobson gave Harris permission to publish a letter which he wrote to him on 15 January 1986:

There remains the issue of whether the 'cellars under the church' in which Rebecca alleges she is sheltering at the time of the massacre of the Jews at the castle of York can be proved to have existed in 1190. The answer to this can only be a definite negative, for it now seems overwhelmingly most likely that the chamber which workmen reported encountering when renovating St Mary's Castlegate in 1975 was not an early medieval crypt at all but a post-medieval charnel vault ... The fact that this vault or chamber remains inaccessible in January 1986 must not, in my opinion, persuade anyone into believing that Rebecca's reference to cellars under a church adds any authenticity to her story. The evidence available is now revealed as so weak in this instance that it fails to support any thesis which suggests that Rebecca's regression contains within it genuine and direct memories of late 12th-century York.

Jeffrey Iverson admitted he was puzzled by one aspect of Jane Evans' memories of being Alison in medieval France:

How is it that this girl can know Coeur had an Egyptian bodyslave and not be aware that he was married with five children – a fact published in every historical account of Coeur's life? If the explanation for the entire regression is a reading of history books in the 20th century, then I cannot explain how Bloxham's subject would not know of the marriage.

Melvin Harris came up with the answer – a 1948 novel, *The Moneyman*, by C.B. Costain – which he says 'is based on Coeur's life and provides almost all of the flourishes and authentic-sounding touches' in Jane Evans' past-life memories. Significantly, the novel does not refer to his wife and children and Costain explained why in a brief introduction:

I have made no mention of Jacques Coeur's family for the reason that they played no real part in the events which brought his career to its climax ... When I attempted to introduce them into the story they got so much in the way that I decided finally it would be better to do without them.

So without realising she was doing it and apparently unaware that she had even read Costain's book, Jane Evans' subconscious mind had dressed up the wealth of detail she had once absorbed from a historical novel in order to 'become' one of its characters.

A Novel Explanation of Livonia's Life

Another writer who is largely sceptical of the evidence for reincarnation is Ian Wilson, whose book on the subject, *Mind Out Of Time?*, was published in 1981. At that time, although he believed past-life regressions could largely be explained as cryptomnesia based on historical novels, he regarded the task of tracing the actual literary and other sources of subjects' alleged reincarnation memories as too much of a 'needle in a haystack' exercise to be practicable, but he says:

> I reckoned without the assiduousness of BBC writer and presenter Melvin Harris ... an enthusiastic browser in secondhand bookshops [who] during the last year has tracked down several historical novels that either influenced or directly inspired what have hitherto been regarded among reincarnationists as particularly convincing cases of 'past-life' memories.

Among these was the discovery of a novel which clearly inspired yet another of Jane Evans' lives, that of Livonia in Roman Britain in the late fourth century AD. Ian Wilson brought this to his readers' attention in a later edition of his book, in which he published an additional chapter, 'Cryptomnesia – a Special Postscript', giving a side-by-side comparison of descriptions from Iverson's book, including names of people and places, and those which appear in German-born Louis de Wohl's *The Living Wood* (published in hardback in 1947 and as a paperback under the title *The Empress Helena* in 1960). Wilson adds:

It is important to note that while Constantine, Helena, Constantius, Allectus, Carausius and Osius are all characters known to history, although not necessarily in exactly the circumstances portrayed, Hilary, Valerius and Curio, who all appear in Jane Evans' regression, are entirely fictitious characters invented by De Wohl.

Livonia herself – the apparent past-life persona of Jane Evans – makes just a fleeting appearance in De Wohl's novel, where she appears as a lady-in-waiting who he describes as 'a charming creature with pouting lips and smouldering eyes'.

SOURCES REVEALED BY SUBJECTS

There is a much easier way of discovering whether a hypnotically produced past-life memory is the result of cryptomnesia than scouring secondhand bookshops. You can *ask* the subject while they are hypnotised. Dr Edwin S. Zolik, whose interest in the subject was inspired by the Bridey Murphy story, did his own research at Marquette University in the 1950s. One of his students, a 32-year-old married student of Irish descent, agreed to be hypnotised and revealed a past life in which he was a British soldier, Brian O'Malley, serving in the Irish Guard in County Cork. He had been thrown from a horse and died in 1892. Four days later, Dr Zolik hypnotised him again and asked him to trace the source for his past-life identity. After some hesitation he explained that his grandfather had spoken to him about O'Malley: they had served together in the army.

Taking this research one step further, ten years later, Reima Kampman, a psychiatrist at the University of Oulo, Finland, began an in-depth study which suggested that past-life memories were a mixture of cryptomnesia and fantasy. He discovered that past-life recall was a comparatively common hypnotic phenomenon, and that those who can produce such memories are mentally healthier than those who cannot. One of Dr Kampman's subjects was a fifteen-year-old girl, first hypnotised in 1968, who remembered five lives. In one she was a seven-year-old boy whose father, Aitmatov, was the captain of a small boat. She named the lake on which he worked and said she had died when she fell in while imitating the fish she saw swimming alongside. The subject was told she would not remember what she had said about this life when she came out of hypnosis. Dr Kampman then re-hypnotised her and asked her to go back in her present life to the moment when she first came across the information she used to create the past-life memory. She then revealed that it was based on a novel she had read many years ago.

Dr Kampman checked these details and found that not only the plot and the name of the lake were the same but the author's name was Aitmatov, which she had used as her past-life father. A more detailed account of this research is to be found in D. Scott Rogo's excellent *The Search for Yesterday*, in which he tells us:

> 'In the light of these and several similar cases, Dr Kampman is sceptical of all reincarnation claims. His overall conclusion is that any type of past-life memory is based on hidden information stored in the brain or on symbolised references to traumatic events experienced in one's current life.

MULTIPLE PERSONALITIES

Even though some of the most often-quoted cases of hypnotic regression have been conclusively shown to be the result of cryptomnesia, it would be premature for us to dismiss all such cases, as we shall see in later chapters. In examining such evidence, however, we are dealing with the human mind and its extraordinary powers, and we need to make allowances for this. Take, for example, the remarkable ability of the mind to 'become' different people, as in cases of multiple personality disorder (MPD). In these, an individual will apparently talk, behave and think like a different person and even have a name for that personality who might manifest suddenly, stay 'in possession' of the subject's body for a period of time, then disappear, to be replaced either by the subject's normal self or by yet another multiple personality. It is said that there are

300,000 sufferers from this condition in the USA alone, and one of the most extreme cases is Donna Smith who was diagnosed as being an MPD sufferer at the age of nineteen. She has sixty-five personalities.

There are many astonishing cases of multiple personality disorder on record, including one in which one of the characters was allergic to cats and manifested a very strong reaction if a cat came near. These symptoms vanished, however, as soon as another personality 'took over'.

Astonishingly, in a recent case, a number of multiple personalities were sworn in and allowed to testify during a trial. A married supermarket worker in Oshkosh, Wisconsin, USA, was charged with sexually assaulting a 27-year-old woman, named only as Sarah, who had forty-six separate 'selves'. He maintained that consent had been given. During her court appearance, Sarah closed her eyes and paused as she moved between personalities at the request of the District Attorney, Joseph Paulus. The judge, Robert Hawley, required the woman to take an oath each time she changed personalities and the lawyers formally introduced themselves to the different identities. Among the six personalities who testified through Sarah during the trial was a six-year-old girl, 'Emily', who was also said to have been assaulted, and a man named 'Sam'. The accused, Mark Peterson, was found guilty of second-degree sexual assault for raping one of the personalities, 'Jennifer', a promiscuous rock fan who liked dancing. But that verdict was subsequently quashed on the grounds that he had not received a fair trial because his psychiatrist was not allowed to examine the woman. A retrial was ordered but Peterson was subsequently freed by the judge after the prosecutor said a retrial would exacerbate the woman's mental condition.

In another celebrated case, that of Sybil Dorsett, sixteen very impressive personalities emerged, including a builder, a carpenter, a writer and a musician. Incredibly, the writer and musician became friends and manifested in Sybil's body in order to have long conversations or even to attend plays and concerts, during which they discussed the proceedings – to the annoyance of other members of the audience. The book *Sybil* and the movie based on it are about this case.

Fascinating though such cases are, because they show the incredible power of the brain, there is no suggestion that multiple personalities constitute past-life memories. They do not have separate identities or histories that can be checked; they are simply fragments of the sufferer's personality and are believed to be the mind's way of coping with abuse or some other trauma.

POSSESSED BY AN 'ANGEL'

The early stages of Mary Lurancy Vennum's mental illness seem to have been typical of MPD, though the syndrome was unknown at the time these events occurred – in 1877. Mary Lurancy Vennum, of Watseka, Illinois, USA, was then thirteen and became 'possessed', at first by a sullen old hag and then by a young man who had run away from home. Hearing of the case, a Mr Roff referred her family to a hypnotist, Dr E. Winchester Stevens, who was able to get through to the teenage girl's 'sane and happy mind'. She told him that 'an angel' named Mary Roff wanted to take the place of the other two personalities – and that's precisely what happened, except that she replaced Mary Lurancy Vennum completely. What is more, Mary Roff had been a real person – the daughter of the man who had referred her family to the hypnotist – who had died when Mary Lurancy Vennum was a year old. Mr and Mrs Roff managed to persuade the girl's parents to allow her to live with them (which was not so surprising, since she no longer recognised them). As far as everyone was concerned, she *was* now Mary Roff and she remained Mary Roff for three months and ten days, at which point Mary Lurancy Vennum took over her body once more and she returned to her parents.

This, it seems, was a case of short-lived spirit possession (as opposed to multiple personality disorder) and provided the Roffs with the comfort of knowing that, somehow, the spirit of their dead daughter still survived and had been able to live with them again for a short period. It's an unusual situation but not unique. There are many modern parallels, including cases where the possession appears to be permanent.

THE STRANGE CASE OF SUMITRA

Take, for example, Sumitra Singh, a young, married woman living with her in-laws in Sharifpura village in the Farrukhabad District of Uttar Pradesh, India. Sumitra had married Jagdish Singh in 1981 at the age of thirteen and given birth to a son in December the following year. But two or three months after the birth she started suffering from fits during which she appeared to go into a trance and speak as if she were someone else. The individuals who seemed to speak through her were a goddess named Santoshi Ma; a woman from the same village, named Munni Devi, who had drowned; and a man from another state who could not be identified. Then, on 16 July 1985, while possessed by the goddess, Sumitra predicted that she would die within three days, and that is precisely what seemed to happen. Her death was witnessed by her family and the villagers on 19 July, but, after having been apparently lifeless and without a pulse for about forty-five minutes, and just as her tearful relatives started preparing for her funeral, she revived.

Sumitra looked around her, was clearly confused and seemed not to recognise anyone. A day later she explained why. She was no longer Sumitra. Her name was Shiva, a mother of two, who had lived in Dibiyapur and been murdered by her in-laws. During a quarrel, she explained, her sister-in-law had hit her with a brick and her family then carried her body to the railway track so that it would appear she had been killed by a train. Gradually more details of Shiva's life emerged, including her father's name and the fact that he was a teacher living in Etawah.

What was particularly upsetting for those concerned was that Sumitra refused to recognise her husband and son and insisted that she wanted to go back to her own two children. Sumitra's family at first thought she had gone mad, then decided she had become possessed by a spirit. They made no attempts to verify her statements. Eventually, Sumitra agreed to resume normal relations with her husband and to care for her child but still insisted she was Shiva.

Dr Satwant Pasricha, India's best-known reincarnation researcher, heard about the case in November 1985 and began investigating it within three weeks. She discovered that, since the change in her personality, Sumitra had begun addressing members of her family in a more respectful way, dressed differently and was also able to read and write Hindi with greater ability than before. Three months before Dr Pasricha's visit to Sumitra's village, a lecturer at an intermediate school in Etawah, Ram Siya Tripathi, whose married daughter Shiva had died in Dibiyapur, heard a rumour that his daughter had been reborn in Sharifpura and decided to find out for himself. He and one of Shiva's maternal uncles, Baleshwar Prasad, arrived in Sharifpura in October 1985 and introduced themselves to Sumitra's in-laws at the door. They were invited in and Sumitra is said to have recognised her father immediately, calling him 'Papa' as Shiva did, and weeping bitterly. She recognised Baleshwar Prasad also, and identified fourteen people in photographs which they had brought with them. This visit convinced Ram Siya Tripathi that Sumitra had the memories of his daughter and he asked her in-laws to allow her and her husband to visit him in Etawah the following day. There she recognised other members of Shiva's family who were not in the photographs – bringing the total to twenty-two – including an uncle who she correctly named and said was from Kanpur. That was where he lived and had his business during Shiva's life but he had since moved back to Etawah.

Shiva had been well educated, up to university level, and it was possibly her superior education and urban manners which caused friction with her husband's family with whom she lived. What is beyond dispute is that she had a serious quarrel with her in-laws after they refused to allow her to attend the marriage of a member of her sister's family. Next day, on 19 May 1985, at the age of twenty-two, her body was found on the railway track and her in-laws claimed she had thrown herself in front of a train. By 11 a.m. she had been cremated.

She may have committed suicide but there were strong suspicions that she had been murdered and Ram Siya Tripathi instigated a judicial inquiry on the matter. Some sceptics might argue that Sumitra or her family could have learned of Shiva's violent death through newspaper reports but that does not explain the sixteen details that could be confirmed about Shiva and her family which did not appear in any published accounts.

Only time will tell if Shiva has taken up permanent residence in Sumitra's body, and whether the soul of Sumitra has gone into another dimension or has been reborn. But, from a spiritual viewpoint, it does not matter whether this is a case of reincarnation or spirit possession. Whichever interpretation is accepted, it seems to provide remarkable evidence that we each have a spirit which survives physical death in a form that enables it to carry, from body to body, the memories and emotions of a former life.

chapter twelve

SICK OF THE PAST

THE TORTURE VICTIM

*F*or thirteen years Carol Lawson, a successful business-woman in Hampshire, England, was plagued by a disfiguring problem which defied medical treatment. Her thumbs would become sore and swollen, and then the nails would fall off. New nails would slowly grow in their place but the same condition recurred at six-monthly intervals. This caused Carol Lawson some difficulties since she also did modelling at that time and is still involved with a model agency. Though the doctors suggested that she might be suffering from a form of dermatitis, the creams they prescribed did nothing to help the unsightly condition.

Then, early in 1994, she stumbled on a cure quite by accident. As well as her business interests, Carol Lawson is also a clairvoyant whose readings had aroused media interest in the south of England. She had a reputation for being willing to speak out on spiritual and psychic matters and so, when Meridian Television were looking for a volunteer to be hypnotised back to a past life, as part of a programme hosted by Dr Hilary Jones, they invited her to take part.

London hypnotherapist Miles Austin conducted the regression in which she gave a vivid and tearful account of her life and death in Atlantis, the legendary island which is said to have disappeared beneath the waves many thousands of years ago. Off camera, Carol found that she and Miles had much in common, including the same birthday, and they agreed to keep in touch. In fact, he phoned her the next day to make sure that she was all right after the regression and learned that her right eye was weeping. The drops which the doctor had prescribed were not easing the problem; it was as if she were still shedding tears for her life on Atlantis. Miles Austin was able to tell Carol Lawson what mental exercises to do to overcome the problem and the tears soon stopped. But he was also intrigued by her nail problem and she agreed to undergo a further hypnotic regression to see if it would throw light on the condition.

'Up until that time, even though I was involved in spiritual work, I never gave any thought to reincarnation,' she told me, when I interviewed her for a feature in our columns. 'I don't know whether I believed or not. It certainly had never occurred to me that my nail condition might have a past-life cause.'

During the regression she recalled being a Cockney woman named Mary and a Native American Indian male with a daughter named White Star.

'Then we went back to Melissa. She lived over 380 years ago and worked in the fields but only when the sun shone.' Carol Lawson spoke with a West Country accent as she described events in that life and the regular appearance of a carriage containing a grand person – possibly royalty – which passed through the village. One day, however, she saw all the men get onto their horses and depart. Curiosity got the better of her, she took a small bag of food and, following in the same direction as the men of the village, she walked to the next town. There she saw the horses tied up outside a building from which dreadful screams were coming. Peering inside when a soldier's back was turned, she saw a man in a long red and gold robe who was being tortured. He, she knew, was the person who passed by in the carriage. At this point she was caught by the soldiers who began pulling her long hair. 'It's funny,' she observes, 'but in this life I've never been able to wear my hair long.'

She was taken inside the building where there were bodies everywhere and they applied a thumbscrew to each hand. 'It was made of iron and was dirty and horrid. I felt a tingling in my hands and fingers and my arms going numb, as I relived the torture. It was horrible. Then the soldiers took Melissa outside and she was hanged.'

Remarkably, the act of remembering those cruel events in 1613 seems to have had a therapeutic effect. One explanation is that the misery inflicted on her past self left such an impression on her psyche that the damage it did was able to manifest once more in a totally different body. For, ever since the regression, the condition has improved dramatically. Over a two-and-a-half year period she lost her nails just once, but she is pleased about that because she has been able to preserve them as proof of her story.

In the middle of 1996, Carol Lawson agreed to be regressed again by Miles Austin so that *Reader's Digest* could film Melissa's memories for a video on the paranormal. During that session they learned a little more about the Englishwoman's life and violent death, but returning to that life seems to have disturbed the healing process. Soon afterwards, the nails began to swell and deteriorate slightly. They have not been shed and Carol is hopeful that they will soon return to normal. 'But I've decided I won't go back to being Melissa again.'

I could quote hundreds of other cases in which regression therapy has proved beneficial for the patients concerned, often resulting in complete cures even when their condition had failed to respond to years of conventional treatment. It would seem from these cases that we bring into this life the fears, guilt or even disabilities from which we suffered in a former life and that only by understanding this can we come to terms with the condition and overcome it. Unlike the case of Carol Lawson, however, most of the published accounts are anonymous, having come from the casebooks of professional therapists whose code of ethics prohibits them from naming their patients.

What is beyond dispute is that thousands of people are being helped, mainly in the West, by consulting past-life therapists and 'removing' barriers in their present life by recalling what appear to be previous incarnations. This statement is not based only on the claims of past-life therapists; there are others who have no belief in reincarnation who are prepared to testify.

Almost anyone working with hypnosis for therapeutic

purposes is likely to stumble across past-life memories at some time, whether they like it or not and regardless of their belief or scepticism about reincarnation. Without being told to go back in time to a previous existence, there are some individuals who will do so of their own accord in response to what is a fairly open-ended suggestion by the hypnotist. In fact, many of today's most successful past-life therapists were introduced to the subject by a patient who did just that. They usually greet this phenomenon with scepticism initially but that response is soon replaced by enthusiasm when they see their patient improve dramatically as a result of his or her memories.

RESOLVING SEXUAL PROBLEMS THROUGH HYPNOTHERAPY

Dr M. Gerald Edelstein, who was staff psychiatrist at Herrick Memorial Hospital in Berkeley, California, at the time he wrote his book *Trauma, Trance and Transformation* in 1981, is not a believer in reincarnation but has witnessed firsthand the spontaneous emergence of past-life memories during conventional hypnotherapy. He reveals in his book that, after using the 'affect bridge' (a technique which is particularly effective when dealing with behavioural problems), he has found that some patients appear to go back, under hypnosis, to another life. The therapist who experiences this phenomenon then helps the patient to deal with the memory and resolve it and improvement usually follows. 'These experiences, for reasons I cannot explain, almost always lead to rapid improvements in the patients' lives,' he writes.

He quotes the case of a legal secretary named Shirley, a woman in her late thirties who was having sexual difficulties with her husband. She did not find sex enjoyable except by engaging in violent rape fantasies. Using his normal hypnotherapy techniques, Dr Edelstein asked her to go back in time to the point where she first associated sex with violence. She responded by describing a scene in which she was a baby watching her mother bleed to death as a result of her birth. This puzzled him since he had already established, in discussions with Shirley, that her mother had entered a tuberculosis clinic two years after giving birth to her. So he asked her what year it was and she replied '1793'. She then said her father was a trapper, the family lived in a log cabin and a neighbour had acted as midwife during the birth.

Needless to say, this revelation surprised patient and doctor. The fact that her relationship with her husband also improved was even more mystifying, for it had not responded to any other form of therapy. On the debit side, however, Shirley presented Dr Edelstein with a new problem. She was now scared that her improvement might hurt someone or that she herself would be hurt.

During another hypnotic session Shirley went back to another past life, in nineteenth-century France, where she attended a ball while her sick husband stayed at home. There she met a man and a brief affair followed. Her husband died soon after learning of the affair and she blamed herself for his death. This apparent past-life memory had more significance for the patient than for the doctor, for she was able to report at her next session that she had lost the feeling that her love-making could hurt someone.

The next hypnotic session produced a memory of a life in fifteenth-century Spain where she had been raped by her father. That recall had the effect of ridding her of her final anxiety, the fear that she herself would be hurt, and Dr Edelstein was able to discharge her as cured. But how had this result been achieved?

Dr Edelstein suggested a number of possibilities derived from the theory that the past-life memories were based on traumatic childhood dreams. And, although he said, 'I do not accept reincarnation for this case,' Edelstein admitted that conventional psychological theory could not explain it either. 'It is entirely conceivable to me that … some theory, as yet unannounced, may lead to be better understanding.'

THE EXTRAORDINARY POWER OF PAST-LIFE THERAPY

The technique's efficacy in dealing with stubborn conditions is confirmed by those working with it on a day-to-day basis. Dr

Roger Woolger, an Englishman now based in the USA and author of *Other Lives, Other Selves*, says that past-life regression 'is one of the most concentrated and powerful tools available to psychotherapy short of psychedelic drugs'.

Another past-life therapist, Dr Edith Fiore, comments: 'Other therapies address the symptoms and leave the cause untouched. Past-life therapy attacks the root cause. There isn't a single physical problem that can't be resolved by good past-life treatment.'

One of the pioneers of past-life therapy, Hazel Denning, who has been practising it for over forty years, echoes those sentiments:

> I believe that past-life regression therapy ... reaches more people, solves more problems faster than any other therapy because it gets to the primary cause and explains the whys. I never have a client that I don't ask. 'What is the spiritual lesson for you in this experience? What is the purpose in this?' They always know.

Dr Denning has also made these observations about past-life therapy:

> I believe I was one of the first to realise that the last emotionally charged thought people have just as they are dying is the thought or emotion they bring with them into the next incarnation. Anger, resentment, fear, guilt – all seem to carry over and manifest even in very small children. 'I can't be trusted', 'I am going to get even with that ...', 'Life is not fair', 'I am a bad person and need to be punished' are examples of the powerful energies that carry over and have to be dealt with in the current incarnation.

Dr Morris Netherton, another pioneer, also believes that it is our deaths in previous lives which cause us the most trouble in this: 'The unresolved trauma of death is a primary cause of behavioural disorder. Most of the problems I encounter have their source in past-life deaths. When the impact of these deaths is erased, many disorders simply evaporate.'

One of the most respected therapists working in this field is Dr Winafred Blake Lucas, a diplomate of the American Board of Professional Psychology, who began her academic training at the University of Washington in the early 1930s, majoring in Greek, philosophy and writing. In addition to her work as a past-life therapist, Dr Blake Lucas spends much of her time teaching and also runs a publishing company which specialises in books on the subject. She is the editor of the impressive two-volume *Regression Therapy, A Handbook for Professionals* which is essential reading for anyone working in the field and also shows the great variety of techniques that can be applied. The following extract from her own contribution to the book gives a valuable insight into the way some individuals come to understand their experiences in their present life in terms of reincarnation:

Intimations of past lives flickered around me from childhood on, but the conditioning of my culture made me blind and deaf to them. At times I wondered about my aptitudes, addictions, deep interests, ancient thoughts; but remaining loyal to the thinking of my time, I denied that they had unseen roots. Still, I found myself puzzling about why contact with any animal, wild or tame, always moved me so deeply that I was choked with tears, and how at eight I could take an unrideable horse and without experience manage it competently. And it was totally inexplicable to me when I was fifteen that I became haunted by the excruciating feeling that I had committed a terrible crime and would be found out and executed, a fear I could leave behind only when I made it to my sixteenth year.

Looking back later, I wondered that I, whose family, though scholarly, had nothing to do with the Classics, began to study Greek at fourteen and found myself able to read Plato at seventeen at a time when Greek had almost disappeared from the universities. And when I began to write a biography of Socrates, I questioned uneasily where all the certain knowledge about him came from that I had not read in any book. A few years later I learned Sanskrit by myself and found that it, too, was my language, and I made my way to Europe during the early thirties to earn a doctorate in it so that I could read the *Vedas* – not the most practical thing to do in a Depression. Intimations of past lives were present constantly, but, not wanting to be out of step with my time, I carefully looked the other way.

The time came, of course, when Winafred Blake Lucas could look away no longer. Her first past-life experiences came when she was a control subject in an LSD experiment in the Medical School at the University of California, Los Angeles. With no warning, she says, 'I was plunged into the deepest perceptions of my life.' These included visions of lives as a child in India, as the wife of a ruler in a small principality near Pakistan in the ninth century, and death in an English cathedral in the fifteenth century. Later, during a workshop on auras, which seemed to put her into an altered state of mind, 'I found myself back in Paris at the time of the French Revolution, lying with my neck on the guillotine in the process of being beheaded.' She tried to scream but no sound came out and she continued with the workshop. Later, standing in the corner of the unattractive classroom, 'I knew in a way of knowing that is difficult to comprehend or explain, that in that life I had been a young woman of twenty-nine and that my daughter in this lifetime was my husband in that one. He had deserted me, and the soldiers had caught me and brought me to my death.'

These insights have enabled Winafred Blake Lucas to develop techniques that she uses to help others who are endeavouring to cope with difficulties which appear to have past-life causes. But are such experiences as real as they seem? One problem we have in answering this question is that the majority of past-life therapists have not the slightest interest in verifying their patients' memories. Why should they? They are consulted by people who want to get better and, if using techniques which produce previous-life accounts results in improvement or cure, then they have achieved all they set out to do. Delving deeper into those memories, perhaps discovering that they were fantasies rather than real events, might only undo the therapy.

FANTASIES BUILT ON TRAUMAS?

Dr Edith Fiore, who says she is 99 per cent convinced that reincarnation is a fact, sees no reason why such research should be carried out.

> Even if every detail given by a patient under hypnosis is shown to be an accurate statement about a person who had once lived, you are not proving the patient actually lived the life. You are just showing that someone lived and died. The patient could be tapping into someone else's thought forms.

Dr Kampman, whose research was discussed in the last chapter, feels that the recollections of past lives produced under hypnosis during therapy sessions are probably fantasies built on a trauma suffered in the patient's present life that is still too threatening to confront directly.

Another medical expert who does not subscribe to the reincarnation interpretation is Dr Lewis Wolberg of New York, an authority on hypnosis and hypnotherapy, who says:

> I have listened to dramatic outpourings of previous lives in many of my patients, and in each instance I was able to trace the tales to forgotten impressions of early childhood, which had been experienced by or told to the subjects.

He believes that such cases are symbolic fantasies constructed in the same way as dreams.

This is a view shared by Professor Ian Stevenson, who says that hypnosis has much in common with dreams and it surprises him that people who attach no importance to their dreams accept hypnotic memories as true.

THE HEALING POWER OF PAST-LIFE THERAPY

The Canadian fashion model Bonnie Brown had suffered with bouts of bronchitis every winter since childhood. Then, at the age of twenty-nine, she was taken back to six different past lives by hypnotherapist Beverley Janus. One of these was as an East European woman, taken with others by Second World War soldiers on a freezing cold train with no food or water. Bonnie coughed throughout this regression memory and had to be wrapped in blankets because she felt so cold. Eventually the train arrived at a camp ringed with barbed wire. Describing that dreadful experience, she said, 'I was coughing blood. I remember thinking: "I don't want to live any more." No one seemed to care. I was coughing and coughing until the end.'

Was this a real memory of a life she had lived before? Or was the beautiful model simply drawing on films she had seen or books she had read about concentration camp atrocities in order to 'explain' her repeated bouts of ill-health? We cannot say with any certainty because this, like most other past-life therapy cases, does not provide sufficient evidence of reincarnation. It does, however, show why past-life therapy is so popular. Beverley Janus told the hypnotised model at the end of the session that she would no longer be affected by the bad experiences of her past. That was in 1972. And when Joe Fisher wrote *The Case for Reincarnation* twelve years later he was able to report that, since then, 'Bonnie hasn't experienced a trace of bronchial trouble'.

The Toronto model says:

I feel that reincarnation is the best explanation for what happened. But if it was only an exploration of my psyche to show me that I no longer need to have bronchitis, who cares? The main thing is that it works.

chapter thirteen

LIFE BETWEEN LIVES

THE SPANISH CARDINAL

The woman who consulted Californian hypnotherapist Hazel Denning was angry and agitated. She banged the arms of the chair and screamed:

I can't stand it any longer. I can't go on living like this. There is no God. Jesus Christ is a fraud. I have prayed, I have studied the Bible, I have had private therapy, group therapy, I have meditated, and nothing does any good.

About the only treatment the woman had not tried was past-life therapy, and when she contacted Hazel Denning, she chose a pioneer in the field. 'You are my last hope,' the well-educated woman emphasised as they prepared to make the first journey back in time to one or more past lives which might shed light on her present troubled life.

First, Hazel Denning got to know the woman better. She learned of the twenty-year marriage which she had longed to terminate but would not because she did not want to admit she had made a mistake. She had set up in business four times, but each time she failed financially and had to start up again. Even her three children had caused her pain as they grew up.

By the fourth hypnotic session Hazel Denning decided it was time for her patient to face a deep-seated feeling of guilt which she had so far been unable to confront. Having assured her that whatever it was she could handle it, the psychotherapist hypnotised her and asked her to go back to the situation which had given rise to these feelings. What happened next is described in Winafred Blake Lucas' *Regression Therapy, Volume II*, a ground-breaking manual for people working with past lives.

'She was a good trance subject and almost immediately began describing a man in a beautiful and ornate garment with a tall headdress,' writes Hazel Denning:

> She said he was a cardinal in the Catholic Church and she then began speaking in the first person. 'I am that person.' In considerable detail she described herself listening to complaints and accusations brought before her, and in a shocked voice she said she was sending many people to the rack. She identified the period as the Spanish Inquisition.

The woman went on to describe some of the events in which she was involved and her feelings about them, adding, 'No wonder I am still feeling guilty about something. I was responsible for killing all those people. No wonder I am still feeling guilty. I *should* suffer for that.'

This seems to be as good a point as any to make an observation about which I feel very strongly. Past-life regression is *not* a game. It should be conducted only by qualified therapists who can handle difficult situations and strong emotions. And it should be tried only by those who have a serious need to resolve inner problems or those whose curiosity is tempered by balanced judgement. The question each person must ask before consulting a past-life therapist is, 'Can I cope with learning that I was a thoroughly unsavoury person in the past?'

In this particular case, the woman concerned could have left the consulting room with a far greater sense of guilt than when she entered. But, with a skilled therapist like Hazel Denning in control, that was not allowed to happen. There are many therapeutic techniques for dealing with traumatic past-life recall, one of which is to ask the subject what lessons he or she has learned from reliving the previous existence. Hazel Denning felt the need to try something new, as she explains:

> When clients have been perpetrators of pain on others in the past, it is not always easy to help them forgive themselves. In this case, where her past deeds had been so horrendous, I knew there had to be a different approach,

so I explained that no human being has that much power over others unless there is a higher motive in progress. I asked her mind to tell her the purpose of the Inquisition.

The woman then said she could see herself in the interlife – the dimension in which our souls reside between each incarnation – talking to a group of spirits and discussing the situation and the condition of the Catholic Church. She learned that the Church was so corrupt at that time that someone 'highly developed in spiritual understanding' had to return to earthly life in order to revolutionise the Church through the Inquisition. She was selected for that role but lost awareness of her spiritual purpose, leaving her with a heavy sense of guilt.

This new insight into her past and present lives apparently left her a 'happy and successful woman'.

AN UNDISCOVERED COUNTRY

This account opens up an area of exploration – an undiscovered country – which is all too often overlooked by those who write about or study reincarnation. In most cases, where we are able to determine both the date of death in a previous life and the birth date in this life, we find a great disparity in the so-called 'intermission period'. There are cases where the time lapse is nine months, from which we could argue that the soul of an individual has entered the embryo virtually from conception. But there are also equally convincing cases where a personality seems to have left one body and been reborn in another in a matter of hours. Generally, however, the period between death and rebirth does not fall neatly into any biological pattern and can be many years apart.

From this we can deduce that the soul is quite capable of living independently of the body, in some spiritual dimension, until the time comes when it must immerse itself in physical matter again and experience a new life. If that is so, then maybe most of the research carried out into past lives so far is not focusing on what really matters. If there is a spiritual dimension to which we all return, again and again, perhaps we could learn far more from examining what happens there, rather than the trials and tribulations of lives spent on earth.

In his extensive studies of children who remember past lives, Professor Ian Stevenson has found that in thirty-two cases from Thailand where the death and rebirth dates were sufficiently reliable to make the calculation, the median interval was sixteen months. The intermission period in Sri Lankan cases was eighteen months and in Burma twenty-one months. Interestingly, in 23 per cent of his Burmese cases, the children not only recalled their past life but also described what they experienced in the interlife state. 'Our ignorance should restrain conjectures about why the subjects of Thai and Burmese cases have (on the average) so much more to tell about experiences during the intermission period than have subjects of other cultures,' he comments. He goes on to observe that:

> Burmese subjects sometimes say they remember being guided to the home of the next rebirth by an elderly sage dressed in white, similar to the 'men in white' described by many subjects in Thailand. And as in Thailand, the Burmese 'men in white' usually act as guides who only indicate the place for rebirth already selected by other processes and do not influence the selection. Sometimes a 'man in white' seems to keep in touch with a person whose rebirth he has guided after the person has been reborn and even throughout the rest of his life. The 'man in white' may sometimes appear in dreams or apparitions to the subject, especially at times of crisis or danger.

SPIRIT GUIDES AND GUARDIAN ANGELS

These descriptions remind us of the spirit guides or guardian angels who many Westerners believe accompany us through life, giving spiritual support and unseen help whenever it is needed. They also bear a striking resemblance to some descriptions given by individuals who have had near-death experiences. As well as seeing loved ones who have died and are waiting for them in the next world, they often see radiant figures, usually dressed in white robes, who they identify either in religious terms or in some other way which acknowledges their wisdom or compassion. These accounts come from people who have had the merest glimpse of that other world before the door has been firmly closed and they have been told their time has not yet come. But hypnotic regression, it seems, enables some individuals to recall in detail what it was like to live in that world at some point in the past.

Toronto-based psychiatrist Dr Joel Whitton was twenty-eight and actively studying hypnotically induced past-life memories when he accidentally stumbled on the interlife – or what Tibetan Buddhists call the *bardo* state. One of his subjects, Paula Considine, could recall a number of lives and it was while taking her from one to another, in April 1974, that he gave an imprecise command. Normally he would instruct his patient to go backwards or forwards to an *incarnation*, but on this occasion he said, 'Go to the life before you were Martha.' Under hypnosis the mind takes instructions very literally and Paula's mind moved to a disembodied life *between* incarnations. She described being 'in the sky' over rural Maryland and watching her mother-to-be, heavily pregnant with the body she would shortly be inhabiting, struggling to pump water into a bucket.

This revelation inspired Dr Whitton to explore the interlife state – which he calls metaconsciousness – with thirty individuals who were particularly good, deep trance subjects. Revealing the results of these experimental ventures into the *bardo* state in his book *Life Between Life*, co-authored by Joe Fisher, he writes:

> Through metaconsciousness, they came to learn *why* they were embroiled in the circumstances of the current incarnation. Furthermore, they realised that they themselves, while discarnate, had actively chosen the setting and involvements of their earthly existence. Parents, careers, relationships and major events contributing to joys and sorrows were seen to have been selected in advance.

What is more, those who recalled time spent in the interlife confirmed that we are each judged on the actions we have taken in our previous incarnation. Their testimony, the book continues,

> thoroughly endorses the existence of a board of judgement and enlarges considerably on the rather sparse descriptions handed down from the old world. Nearly all who ventured into metaconsciousness have found themselves appearing before a group of wise, elderly beings – usually three in number, occasionally four, and in rare instances as many as seven – perceived in a variety of guises. They can be of indeterminate identity or they may take on the appearance of mythological gods or religious masters.

One of Dr Whitton's subjects offered this description:

> My guide took me by the arm and led me to a room where the judges were sitting at a rectangular table. They were all dressed in loose white garments. I sensed their age and their wisdom. In their company, I felt very boyish.

THE MASTER SPIRITS

Dr Brian Weiss, a graduate of Columbia University and Yale Medical School, and Chairman of Psychiatry at the Mount Sinai Medical Center in Miami, might seem an unlikely convert to past-life regression. In fact, he has not only become a champion of rebirth and a leading past-life therapist (see Chapter Six), but he also says that one particular event has changed his life. It happened when a subject entered the inter-life state between incarnations.

One of his patients, Catherine, was a laboratory technician in the hospital where he was chief of psychiatry and had consulted him about various fears and phobias. Dr Weiss had often used hypnosis and found it effective in such cases and eventually persuaded Catherine to try it when she failed to respond to other treatments. What happened next was to provide him with a new and powerful therapeutic tool which he discovered by accident, much like Dr Joel Whitton, when giving his patient an imprecise hypnotic command. He had taken Catherine back to the age of two in this life – at this point he had no interest or belief in past lives – in an attempt to discover the cause of her problems. He then instructed her: 'Go back to the time from which your symptoms arise.' To his astonishment she began describing a life in 1863 BC. Despite his scepticism, reviving these memories after nearly 4,000 years resulted in a total cure. In later hypnotic sessions she recalled being a Spanish prostitute in the eighteenth century and also a Greek woman.

Then, in the fourth or fifth session, something happened which 'completely changed the rest of my life'. Under hypnosis, Catherine entered the interlife where she communicated with highly evolved beings who she described as the Master Spirits. In her trance-like state, Catherine suddenly told Dr Weiss,

> Your father is here, and your son, who is a small child. Your father says you will know him because his name is Avrom, and your daughter is named after him. Also, his death was due to his heart. Your son's heart was also important, for it was backward, like a chicken's. He made a great sacrifice for you out of his love. His soul is very advanced ... his death satisfied his parents' debts. Also he wanted to show you that medicine could only go so far, that its scope is very limited.

Dr Weiss went numb on hearing these words. There was no way that Catherine could have known these personal details about his family but they were all correct. His son Adam had died when he was only twenty-three days old, in 1971, from a heart condition exactly as Catherine had described – which occurs in only one out of every ten million births. His father had died in 1979 and his daughter was named after him.

Catherine revealed that the Master Spirits, as well as giving her this information, had also told her that she had lived eighty-six times in the physical state so far.

'I do not have a scientific explanation for what happened,' writes Dr Weiss in his book, *Many Lives, Many Masters*. 'There is far too much about the human mind that is beyond our comprehension.'

THE BURMESE MONK WHO WAS 'DELIVERED' TO HIS NEW LIFE

This account reminds me of a fascinating past-life memory case in which the individual involved also reported meeting a white-cloaked person. Maung Htwe Nyein was born in November 1921 in Burma and became a senior Buddhist monk, taking the name the Venerable Sayadaw U Sobhana. From a young age he could remember his earlier life as Maung Po Thit, who had a wife named Ma Shwe Thin and a son who was only three years old when he died. After his rebirth, he often went to visit his 'widow' and 'son' who lived close to his former home in the village. And he remembered how he had been guided to the home in which he was to be reborn as the son of the village headman. His death in that past life had occurred after he contracted a severe fever and was taken by oxcart to the hospital where the doctors said he would need an operation:

After that I remember nothing more of the time I spent in hospital. I then found myself in the jungle alone. I was feeling sorrow, hunger, thirst, and great distress, but did not know that I was dead. I was dressed in my usual clothes … I seemed to wander about in the jungle for two or three hours. Then I met a very old man dressed in white with a white beard and moustache and carrying a staff. He was dressed like an *Upasaka* [Buddhist lay devotee] with a white shawl over his shoulder.

When I saw the old man, all my distress vanished. He called me by my name and told me I must follow him. I did so for about an hour, walking. We reached a place I knew near my village. Then we entered the village and went to my house. In front of it there was a fence and a tree. The old man told me to wait there under the tree while he went into the house. I can remember this and can see it all in my mind's eye even now. The memory is very vivid. The old man went into my house and emerged again after five minutes. He said: 'You must follow me to another house.'

We went in a westerly direction. About seven houses distant from my house was the house of the village headman. In front of that house, the old man told me to wait for him. He went inside and returned to me after about five minutes. He called me into the house, and when I was inside he said to me: 'You must stay here. I shall go back.' He then disappeared. I saw people in the house, but after that I remember nothing until I came to consciousness in my present existence.

As soon as he began recalling his past-life memories at a young age, his parents told him what they knew about his death and rebirth. The body of Maung Po Thit had been removed from the hospital and buried. Then, seven days later, a number of monks performed a traditional ceremony for the dead. On that same day, his wife in that former life had a dream in which she saw an old man in white who said: 'I am sending your husband to the village headman's house.' The next morning she ran to the village headman's home and told his wife, Daw Lay Khin, what she had dreamed. Daw Lay Khin revealed that she, too, had dreamed of the same old man in white who told her he was entrusting Maung Po Thit to her family. The headman's wife discovered she was pregnant shortly afterwards and gave birth to a son, the Venerable Sayadaw U Sobhana.

SAI BABA AND THE MAN WHO RETURNED FROM THE DEAD

One of the most astonishing accounts of the interlife was given by an elderly American, Walter Cowan, who was a devotee of Sathya Sai Baba, the Indian guru whom many regard as God incarnate. The story was related by Dr John Hislop, a professor and corporate executive who witnessed the event, and was published in Dr Samuel Sandweiss's *Sai Baba ... The Holy Man and the Psychiatrist*. Walter Cowan died suddenly on Christmas Day 1971 from a heart attack and his body was taken by ambulance to hospital where he was certified dead.

His wife, Elsie, had prayed to Sai Baba for help, ending her prayer, 'Let God's Will Be Done'. Later that day, when she and a friend, Mrs Ratan Lal, went to the hospital they learned that Sai Baba had also visited Walter Cowan. And when they entered his room instead of a corpse they found him alive. Dr Hislop was able to confirm that the American was dead on arrival at hospital and that the doctor who examined him had stuffed his ears and nose with cotton, then covered his body with a sheet.

While all this was going on, Walter Cowan found himself:

very calm, in a state of wonderful bliss; and the Lord, Sai Baba, was by my side. Even though my body lay on the bed, dead, my mind kept working throughout the entire period of time until Baba brought me back. There was no anxiety or fear but a tremendous sense of well-being, for I had lost all fear of death.

Then Baba took me to a very large hall where there were hundreds of people milling around. This was the hall where the records of all my previous lives were kept. Baba and I stood before the Court of Justice. The person in charge knew Baba very well, and he asked for the records of all my lives. He was very kind, and I had the feeling that whatever was decided would be the best for my soul.

Walter Cowan then described armloads of scrolls in many languages being produced and Sai Baba interpreting them. Some concerned countries which had not existed for thousands of years:

When they reached the time of King David, the reading of my lives became more exciting. I could hardly believe how great I apparently was in each life that followed. As the reading of my lives continued, it seemed that what really counted were my motives and character, as I had stood for outstanding peaceful, spiritual, and political activity ...

After about two hours, they finished reading the

scrolls, and the Lord, Sai Baba, said that I had not completed the work that I was born to do and asked the judge that I be turned over to him to complete my mission of spreading the truth. He requested that my soul be returned to my body under his grace. The judge said, 'So be it.'

The case was dismissed and I left with Baba to return to my body. I hesitated to leave this wonderful bliss. I looked at my body and thought it would be like stepping into a cesspool to return to it, but I knew that it was best to complete my mission so that I could eventually merge with the Lord, Sai Baba. So I stepped back into my body ... and that very instant it started all over again – trying to get my breath, being as sick as you could be and still be alive. I opened my eyes and looked at my wife and said, 'You sure look beautiful in pink ...'

THE BOY WHO REFUSED TO BE BORN AGAIN

Not all stories of the interlife are as uplifting as that of Walter Cowan. An English teenager, W. Martin, was knocked unconscious in 1911 by a coping stone and seems to have been close to death. He watched from a disembodied state as people attended his body. Then, against his will, he was carried to a bedroom where a woman was giving birth. He recognised her as a Mrs Wilson. He saw the doctor holding the child in his hands and Martin felt himself almost compelled to press his face through the back of the baby's head. But then he thought of his mother and was immediately drawn to her. He then accompanied his parents to where his body was laid out and climbed into it. With that, he sat up fully conscious, repeating conversations he had heard while out of his body and describing the scene he had witnessed in Mrs Wilson's home. It was discovered later that Mrs Wilson had died at 2.05 p.m. that day after giving birth to a stillborn daughter.

Whatever we make of such stories, they raise the intriguing

possibility that the interlife might be the *real* world and our earthly existences might represent no more than occasional opportunities to further our spiritual education.

chapter fourteen

IN THE WRONG BODY?

THE JAPANESE SOLDIER

Ma Tin Aung Myo was typical of a young Burmese man: wearing a Western-style shirt together with the traditional ankle-length, check-patterned *longyi*, and going steady with local girls near the village of Na-Thul. But Ma Tin Aung Myo was different. She was a woman.

The story she and her family tell is unusual because she not only recalls being a person of the opposite sex but also of another nationality. Ma Tin Aung Myo says she was a Japanese soldier in her past life.

Why should a Japanese soldier be reborn into the body of a Burmese girl? That's a question I cannot answer, except to say that the Japanese Army occupied Ma Tin Aung Myo's village soon after they invaded Burma in 1942. Allied fighter aircraft then began bombing the area, sometimes twice a day, and machine-gunning anyone they saw on the ground, in order to defend Puang railway station nearby which was of strategic importance. Understandably, the Burmese inhabitants chose to escape these attacks by departing from their villages in the morning and returning at night, leaving just the Japanese occupation force in the firing line.

It was an Allied attack, said Ma Tin Aung Myo, that had ended her previous life. She could remember very clearly being a Japanese soldier about to cook a meal near an acacia tree, some 228 feet (75 metres) from the house in which Ma Tin Aung Myo was later born. He was wearing only shorts and a big belt when he was spotted by a pilot who dived at him and began spraying him with machine gun bullets. The soldier ran behind a pile of firewood in the hope of escaping but was struck in the groin and died immediately.

Ma Tin Aung Myo was four when she became scared of aircraft flying overhead. The first time she told her father, 'I want to go home. I want to go home,' and thereafter cried whenever she saw one. Asked why, she explained that they would shoot her. On other occasions she became depressed and wept for no apparent reason. When asked why, she explained, 'I am pining for Japan.'

She then gradually told the family what she could remember about her past life in Northern Japan in which she had five children, the eldest of whom was a boy. The infant Ma Tin Aung Myo often expressed a longing to return to Japan and was clearly uncomfortable with Burma's hot climate and spicy food. As she grew up, however, her past-life memories faded and she became more tolerant of Burmese conditions.

One aspect of her personality did not change, however. From an early age Ma Tin Aung Myo had insisted on wearing boys' clothes and having her hair cut short. When Professor Stevenson interviewed her in 1974, by which time she was twenty-one, she boasted that she did not possess a single item of Burmese women's clothing. As a child she liked being with boys, particularly playing soldiers, and used to ask her parents for toy guns. She also liked playing football.

Her father was more indulgent than her mother in such matters, particularly about the clothes she wore. But her desire to dress like a boy created problems when she was in the sixth grade at school and the authorities insisted that she dress as a girl. Ma Tin Aung Myo refused. The school insisted. And so she dropped out. Thereafter, her parents made no further objections to her wearing masculine clothes.

In her late teens she began to associate more with girls and was well accepted by them, though they addressed her as 'Ko' – a male term – rather than 'Ma', the female honorific.

By 1977, Ma Tin Aung Myo had completely rejected a female position in society and her mother, U Win Maung, reported that she had 'got into the habit of "going steady" with girlfriends'.

So strong was her identification with being male that she

told researchers studying her case that they could kill her by any method they cared to choose on just one condition: that they guaranteed she would be reborn as a boy.

'We had no wish to carry out the first of her stipulations,' they remarked, 'and no power to implement the second.'

Just as he suggests that reincarnation should be considered as an explanation for the transfer of skills from one life to another, so Professor Ian Stevenson believes that those working in the field of sexual identity confusion should also consider past-life influences as a possible cause. He comments:

> The simplest explanation sometimes *is* the best one and I believe that Western psychiatrists and psychologists should seriously consider and investigate further the basis for the Southeast Asian interpretation of cases of gender dysphoria.

Though the case of Ma Tin Aung Myo lacked corroboration, there *is* very impressive past-life evidence in similar cases. Interestingly, the best of these appear to be girls who would rather be boys.

THE BOY STUDENT REBORN AS A GIRL

The first indication that Dolon Champa Mitra was different from other children was when she started wearing boys' clothes at the age of three-and-a-half. The daughter of a superintendent in the Poultry and Dairy Section of the Ramakrishna Mission Ashram in Narendrapur, Sri Lanka, she was found by her mother one day wearing her older brother's shirt and pants. Kanika Mitra told her off and later, when she asked Dolon to rest by her side, the child replied: 'No ... you scold me for wearing a shirt and pants. I was a little bigger boy in a house like a palace.'

Her mother's startled response was: 'What are you saying?', to which her daughter replied: 'Yes, Mother, I am speaking the truth. I had a younger brother and sister. I had a fat aunt and my mother was called Baudi. Take me near the Maharajah's palace and I shall lead you to the house.' She said the place where she had lived was Burdwan, which is a city northwest of Calcutta.

Her curious parents eventually gave in to these pleadings but Dolon was unable to locate the house on her first attempt and they returned home. She insisted on being taken back and her parents eventually obliged on 30 March 1972, helped by some colleagues of the girl's father who knew Burdwan. This time she was successful in finding the house and she, her mother and two other women were invited in. Dolon recognised several of the women in the house and various rooms and objects when she toured the building. It became obvious to everyone that she was remembering the life of Nishith De, a young man who had died in 1964. The boy's mother – who was present – was clearly unhappy about this sudden intrusion, perhaps because her son had apparently returned as a girl. She pushed Dolon away when she approached her and told the girl's mother, 'Let your daughter remain yours,' before walking off and locking herself in her room. These actions clearly upset the girl and the lack of co-operation on the part of the parents of the young man she claimed to have been made corroboration more difficult. But other members of Nishith De's family did co-operate and furnished confirmation of most of Dolon's statements.

The De family were business proprietors and among the richest in Burdwan. Their son, Nishith De, was born in 1940 and was a student studying at Burdwan Raj College when, at the age of twenty-four, he developed a brain disease which quickly deteriorated. He died on 25 July 1964 after being in a coma for fifteen days.

The amount of evidence provided by Dolon Champa Mitra in this case is impressive, but I intend to concentrate on the aspect of sexual-identity confusion. As we have already seen, the young girl began dressing in her older brother's clothes at an early age and liked to wear a shirt and short pants. She did, however, wear dresses to school and it seemed likely that her past-life sexual identity would not have such a powerful influence on her, when she reached puberty, as it apparently had on Ma Tin Aung Myo.

REBORN AS A WOMAN BECAUSE HE EXPLOITED WOMEN?

Rani Saxena also had very clear memories of the previous life she had lived as the son of a prosperous lawyer in Benares, India. Born to parents of far more modest means in Allahabad, she identified very strongly with her former life at an early age and displayed many masculine traits. These continued into middle age, by which time she had married (by a family arrangement) and produced two children. Despite that, and the fact that she was undoubtedly a good though reluctant mother, she still used masculine verb forms. (In Hindi, some verb forms indicate the speaker's sex.) It was Rani Saxena's belief that God had put her into a female body and given her a life of comparative poverty because in her former life as a male lawyer she had selfishly exploited women.

BORN A GIRL AT LAST

Gnanatilleka Baddewithana, on the other hand, could remember that in her previous life as a boy she had wanted to be a girl and this wish was clearly granted. What is more, when investigators checked her story, this unusual aspect appeared to be confirmed.

Born at Hedunawewa in Sri Lanka (then Ceylon) on 14 February 1956, Gnanatilleka began talking about her past life when she was only two, saying she had a mother and father in another place and also two brothers and many sisters. She eventually named the village in which she had lived as Talawakele and gave other details including names. From this information it was established that she was referring to a family who had lost a thirteen-year-old son named Tillekeratne in November 1954. Subsequently, when the two families met, she was able to recognise various people, including her previous parents. She also developed a close relationship with D.V. Sumithapala, a teacher who had taken a special interest in Tillekeratne at his school, and who could remember the boy asking him if it was true that after we die we are reborn and also if it were possible for a boy to be reborn as a girl. At times

Gnanatilleka's fondness and veneration of her former-life teacher exceeded that which she showed for her parents.

She eagerly awaited his visits and Sumithapala returned her affection warmly. He said that he became tearful when she first recognised him at the time of his first visit to her at Hedunawewa in 1960. He was a witness of her recognitions of the family and friends of Tillekeratne in Talawakele and when she became excited he comforted her. He had continued to visit her regularly since then.

The teacher fully believed that the boy he had once taught had been reborn as Gnanatilleka, as did Tillekeratne's mother. Gnanatilleka's own parents also shared that belief and were worried that she might carry out her threat, uttered in moments of petulance, to return to 'my Talawakele mother'.

As well as Tillekeratne's reported question to his teacher about the possibility of being reborn as a girl – suggesting perhaps that it was something he desired – his mother and his schoolteacher said that Tillekeratne had developed a definite tendency toward effeminacy. This showed itself in a marked preference for the society of girls over boys ... 'an interest in sewing, a fondness for silk shirts and, on occasion, painting his fingernails.' Although a male painting his fingernails is not viewed in such an extreme way in Sri Lanka as it is in the West, it is nevertheless regarded as an indicator of effeminacy and Tillekeratne was the only boy his teacher, D.V. Sumithapala, ever saw doing this.

Gnanatilleka also said she was happier now that she was a girl than in her previous life. She displayed some masculine tendencies in this life at an early age but they were never very prominent and they soon disappeared as she developed normally as a female.

'WHY DID I BECOME A GIRL?'

In another Sri Lankan case, Ruby Katsuma Silva began talking about a previous life before she was two years old. The youngest of nine children, seven of whom were brothers, she was born at Galle in September 1962, the daughter of a clerk at Batapola post office. Having seven sons and just one daughter, the addition of another daughter to the family was greeted with delight by her parents. But as soon as she could talk Ruby insisted that she had been a 'brother' not a 'sister' and acted like a boy. She even asked, 'Why did I become a girl?'

She told her parents she had lived in the town of Aluthwala, had attended religious school at its temple, and had worked in the paddy fields. One day, on returning from the fields, she had gone to a well to wash but had fallen in and drowned. Not having the vocabulary to describe this event at a tender age, Ruby used gestures to help explain what had happened. Ruby's mother went to the temple to make enquiries and, with the help of its monks, discovered that a family named Singho had lost a son, Karunasena, in the manner described in July 1959, when he was seven-and-a-half years old.

When news reached Karunasena's family a number of them decided to visit Ruby at Pollewa and she recognised everyone who would have been known to Karunasena. In fact, because they were unknown to members of her own family, Ruby made all the introductions – as if she were the boy.

Like other subjects suffering sexual identity confusion, Ruby's masculine behaviour manifested principally in the clothes she wore and the games she played. She preferred to wear trousers and a shirt and sarong, as she had in her previous life. Even when she wore dresses she wore shorts underneath them. To satisfy this urge she would borrow her brothers' sarongs, shirts and singlets. She was a skilful kite flyer and player of *cadju* (similar to American marbles) and joined boys playing cricket as well as riding her brother's bicycle. Ruby also loved climbing trees, which investigators regarded as the most masculine trait of all, and was fond of whistling. She was inclined to be aggressive in arguments with her brothers. And it was also notable that she had no interest in cooking, which is normally regarded as a feminine skill.

Ruby never asked her family to call her by her past-life names but she did ask repeatedly to be called 'brother' or 'son'. Her mother yielded on this point in 1968 but the children called her 'brother' only when they were angry with her.

The change of sex from one life to the next clearly puzzled

Ruby and she told her mother on one occasion that when she died she wanted to be reborn as a boy again.

DO WE ALTERNATE BETWEEN SEXES?

In hypnotic regressions to apparent past lives, subjects often alternate between sexes and appear to accept such changes without surprise or embarrassment. Whether such memories are real, mental fantasies or wish-fulfilment is an open question. But, according to the scientific study of past-life cases, mainly with children who are born with apparent memories of previous incarnations, a change from one sex to another is rare.

'In total of some 600 cases, differences of sex between the two personalities have occurred in only about 5 per cent,' Professor Stevenson reports. He also notes that the proportion of such sex-change cases varies enormously from one culture to another in a way which accurately reflects their beliefs. For example, it occurs in half the cases he has studied among the Kutchin (Athabaskan) of the Canadian Northwest Territories, yet is totally absent in Lebanon, Turkey, and among the tribes of southeastern Alaska (the Tlingit) and British Columbia (the Haida, Tsimsyan and Gitksan). Elsewhere, it ranges between 28 per cent in Burma, 15 per cent in the (non-tribal) United States, and 13 per cent in Thailand, to 9 per cent in Sri Lanka, and 3 per cent in India. Why?

Professor Stevenson gives the following explanation:

When I question informants of countries where sex-change cases occur, they tell me that sex change from one life to another is possible; but when I question informants of cultures where such cases do not occur, they tell me that it is impossible ... In all but one of the cultures where sex-change cases occur, girls who remember previous lives as males occur three times as often ... as boys who remember previous lives as females. Since this lopsided ratio appears so consistently, it might almost be regarded as one of the 'universal' features of the cases, although one restricted to cultures where sex-change cases are found.

chapter fifteen

WAR VICTIMS

THE NAZI'S MISTRESS

Swedish-born Lena-Marie Broman struggled to find words to describe the horror of her past-life memories as she addressed a large audience in Norway. Her voice occasionally breaking with emotion, she spoke of the attraction which Vienna had always had for her and also the powerful impact she felt when, at the age of fourteen, she saw her first World War II movie. 'I was overcome by a terrible feeling: I almost fainted.'

But was this the natural repugnance we all feel when faced with war's atrocities, or was she troubled by some deep-rooted trauma? Lena-Marie Broman was not to discover the answer to that question until 1989 when she and her former husband were driving in Sweden along a small road. Their peaceful journey was shattered when they came across a military barracks and she immediately announced, 'There it is!'

Her puzzled husband asked her what she meant but Lena-Marie was unable to reply. She was suddenly engulfed in what appeared to be flashbacks to her previous life.

She later told me:

> I felt myself going straight into a dark tunnel and it was awful. I saw pictures of myself coming with Red Cross buses, and I knew that I had died in a concentration camp. At first I thought it was Dachau but later I discovered it was Buchenwald. I knew that I had two children and they were lost. As we drove on some 100 metres, I took out a mirror because I was crying so much and my make-up was running, and I wanted to compose myself

and put some rouge on my cheeks. Looking in the mirror
I suddenly saw a deep white scar here on my cheek.'

Later, she consulted a psychotherapist, Carl, who regressed her
to her past life and helped her recall some of the events which
had surfaced during the striking experience. Then Lena-Marie
met an anaesthesiologist, Göran Grip, who helped her come to
terms with her past life. Slowly, using hypnosis, they pieced
together the story of that painful life as Anna-Marie
Kellerman, a Jewess married to a musician and the mother of
two children, Naima and Heinz. But she was also the mistress
of Commandant Koch, living at Buchenwald. As the Nazi
atrocities increased, so her son and daughter were taken from
her and then she, too, suffered at the hands of the Germans.

On a visit to Vienna, Lena-Marie even located the apartment where she had lived at one time and produced a drawing
of her father's shop which she was also able to find. But how
evidential is this information?

'We haven't really been looking for factual proof,' Göran
Grip told me after they stepped off the platform at the conference which had been staged to discuss reincarnation. 'We have
been looking for experiences and confirmation of these,
because they are more meaningful, both to me and to Lena-
Marie. Neither of us need factual proof though we did come
across some.' What matters to them is the change which has
been brought about in Lena-Marie as a result of these memories coming to the surface.

Now she says:

> As a child, I did not feel at home with my family: I felt
> like a victim and I have difficulties still in dealing with
> that. It has affected my whole life from the very begin-
> ning. I was a victim in many ways … but no longer. I
> died with guilt for my children and my husband. But now
> I know how to deal with it. Time heals all wounds.

If what Lena-Marie Broman experienced really was the result
of being a Nazi victim in her past-life, think how many more
people – the millions exterminated in the Holocaust – might

have been reborn with the psychological scars of that terrible experience. This was confirmed by another speaker at the Norway conference, Rabbi Yonassan Gershom, an animated, good-humoured man whose book, *Beyond the Ashes*, has introduced new and occasionally controversial ideas and concepts to the reincarnation debate.

JEWISH MYSTICISM AND THE KABBALA

Before we examine Rabbi Gershom's views, here is his explanation of why he, as a Jew, is comfortable with a belief in rebirth:

> Many people are not aware that there are teachings about reincarnation in Jewish mysticism. The Hebrew word is *gilgal*, which comes from the same root as the word circle: it has to do with cycles. So, in a language way, it's similar to the idea of the wheel of karma. This is a teaching which at some point in our history has been relatively mainstream; for instance, during the Middle Ages I would say the majority of Jews in Muslim Spain and northern Africa and in Iran and Iraq – what today are known as Sephardic Jews – would have believed in reincarnation. At this point right now, in the twentieth century, Hasidic Jews, who are the mystical Jews of Eastern Europe, which is my background, also believe in reincarnation. So, there are Jewish teachings on reincarnation but many people in the general public are unaware of it.

Born in California and brought up in Philadelphia, he had neither studied past-life literature nor experimented with regression when he had his first encounter with a person who appeared to be a reborn Holocaust victim. During lectures in Minneapolis on Jewish mysticism – the Kabbala – he noticed an attractive, blonde Scandinavian woman and eventually invited her to join his weekly home study group.

One night there was a snowstorm and he cancelled the class because the roads would be slippery. But she did not live very far away and she did not get the message about the snowstorm. So, when she turned up on his doorstep, Rabbi Gershom said, 'Well, since you're here, you might as well come in, have some coffee, warm up, let's talk, have some dinner.'

They settled down with a coffee and he asked his visitor what she would like to talk about. To his surprise she said, 'the Holocaust'. It transpired that her sister, with whom she was living, was working on a research project on the Holocaust for a university course and kept saying, 'Let me read this material to you.' What she heard horrified her and she wanted to talk about it, but she couldn't handle it. Ever since her childhood, she told Rabbi Gershom, she had had this dreadful fear whenever anyone mentioned Nazis or the Holocaust and she couldn't imagine why, on a rational level, because she had been brought up in rural Minnesota, in a small town, in the middle of the prairie. There were no Nazis there. In fact, there were no Jews either.

As she tried to explain her apparently irrational fears to him, Rabbi Gershom experienced something most unusual. Before he would tell me about it, however, he was at pains to put it into perspective:

I always have to say, at this point, that in the Jewish tradition we don't 'witness' our spiritual experiences. There's very little of the first-hand 'I had a vision'-type literature in the Jewish tradition. It's not because we don't have these experiences, it's because it is considered very egotistical to go around claiming to have visions or dreams or to claim to be a prophet … And the reason I'm saying this is because, I'm going to tell this, but culturally I'm kind of breaking a taboo.

While I was sitting across the table from her I saw another face superimposed on hers, like a double exposure. But both of them were live faces – it wasn't like a still photograph – it was like watching two videos running on top of each other. Her face was this beautiful, young woman with light skin, beautiful blue eyes and long, blonde hair, very nicely made up and attractive like you'd expect to see on the cover of a glamour magazine. Over that face, however, was this very thin, emaciated, starved, painful face with shaved head and sunken eyes and mouth, like a concentration camp victim. The mouths were both moving together and while this was happening I heard a tune in the background and I recognised it right away. It's a tune that comes from Jewish mysticism but it's not something that was well known – not like hearing Yankee Doodle in the background – and she would almost certainly never have been exposed to it.

So I said, 'Look, this might seem a little strange but I think I'm onto something. I'd like to try an experiment. I'm going to hum a tune and see if you recognise it.' She agreed and so I hummed it and it goes like this …

His deep, rich tones produced a melody that is now far better known around the world than at the time of the experience he is relating. The tune comes from the Breslover Hasidim tradition and the words that are sung with it are from Maimonides: 'I believe with perfect faith in the coming of a Messiah, and though I will tarry yet will I believe …'

Rabbi Gershom continues:

It's not clear how it started but some of the Jews in the concentration camps began to sing it as a song of faith. It's known today as 'the hymn of the camps' and the Breslover Hasidim are said to have sung it in defiance as they walked into the gas chambers, knowing they were going to their deaths.

It was sung when Pope John-Paul visited the Synagogue of Rome in the late 1980s and was also used by Steven Spielberg in his powerful film about the Holocaust, *Schindler's List*. Both these events occurred after Rabbi Gershom's encounter with the blonde visitor.

On hearing the song she let out a wail of pain, began to rock back and forth. According to Rabbi Gershom she:

burst into tears and began to sob and describe this scene of the concentration camp and said she'd died there. There was a catharsis, and we spoke for a long time about what she had seen and experienced. She described visions. It wasn't at all an intellectual thing, she went hysterical. She was screaming and crying, almost in trance, staring into space and bawling ... It was as if it were happening right then, to the point that I was saying, 'You're safe, you're OK. Tell me what you see. Pretend it's a movie,' trying to make it shift from physically experiencing it to seeing it. There was so much physical pain and suffering that if someone is experiencing it as if it's happening it can be very frightening.

Eventually, she was able to withdraw and describe what she was seeing and experiencing more objectively. This, says Rabbi Gershom, was the beginning of the healing process which enabled her to overcome her 'Nazi phobia'.

This was just the first of over 200 cases which Rabbi Gershom encountered and which are documented in his book (he has since discovered many more). Since many of these deal with the way in which they died, it is not always pleasant reading, but Rabbi Gershom argues that this is not only justified but necessary:

I do not dwell on these details out of morbidity but to point out that the popular conception of 'six million Jews in gas chambers' does not reflect the many ways in which they were actually killed. Nor does it take into account the tens of thousands of Jews who died of starvation, overwork, disease, suicide, or forced marches. Jews were shot, stabbed, raped, hanged, drowned, disembowelled, dragged behind vehicles, burned, buried alive and killed in medical experiments. One cannot help but be horrified by the fiendish imaginations of the Nazi death squads, who never seemed to lack for new ways to torment their victims.

DO SOULS KEEP THEIR CULTURAL IDENTITY?

Two-thirds of the Nazis' victims identified by Rabbi Gershom at the beginning of his survey had been reborn as non-Jews which inspired a few journalists to use the statistic as a basis for wild speculation, which disturbs him:

> Some people think that if Jews reincarnate as non-Jews it proves that Jews don't have any kind of an identity that carries down over the centuries. It's almost a subtly anti-Semitic thing. I need to stress that it's not only Jews but many other tribal peoples who believe that the soul will reincarnate in the same village, family line, or culture.

He also points out that the sample on which he based his book was mostly from an area of America where there were few Jews. Since publication of his book, 'I've been meeting hundreds of people who were Jews during the Holocaust and are Jews once more in this life. So my figures need to be revised.' But he concedes that it is hardly surprising that some Nazi victims, knowing that they were being put to death just because of their obviously Jewish features, should carry with them into their next life a fear of having dark hair or some other distinctive racial characteristic.

Rabbi Gershom has published a sequel, called *From Ashes to Healing*, which contains 'fifteen true stories' of mystical encounters with the Holocaust. These include Lena-Marie Broman's story, told in greater detail than time permitted at the Norway conference I attended. In it she reveals that soon after she went to a psychotherapist, Carl, she recognised him as the camp commandant who had eventually sent her and her children to their deaths. As in her past life, however, she and Carl became lovers and they now work together in Uppsala, Sweden, helping to heal others.

THE HOLOCAUST AND THE LAWS OF KARMA

Atrocities such as those perpetrated by the Nazis raise important questions about the nature of karma – the so-called spiritual law of cause and effect which is supposed to take account of our good and bad deeds over many lifetimes. The Holocaust presents us with a chicken-and-egg situation, for in ascribing an event to karma one has to make a judgement as to who is the perpetrator and who the victim.

As we saw in Chapter One, Air Chief Marshal Lord Dowding received many angry responses when he declared at a public meeting: 'I have some reason to suppose that those who sowed the seeds of abominable cruelty at the time of the Inquisition reaped their own harvest at Belsen and Buchenwald.'

Among those who rebuked him in the lively newspaper debate that followed his public statement was Hannen Swaffer, a famous English journalist and a firm believer in life after death. He argued that, if Lord Dowding was right, then:

> we must always have cruelty in order that torturers may themselves suffer in their turn. Why, then, strive for human betterment? Why seek to end war? Why work for an ideal social order? If Dowding is right, we are the victims of an immutable law of vengeance to which we must submit. And if he is right, Belsen and Buchenwald were brought into being by God, of whose purpose Hitler and Himmler were the instruments. Nearly 5,000,000 Jews have been exterminated since the war began. Were they all being punished for crimes in some prior existence? If so, the Jewish baiters were right. No! No! No!

Another reader, commenting on the suggestion that the Nazis themselves would be tortured in some future life, observed: 'It follows, then, that the once-tortured, having become torturers, will need to be re-tortured by their original torturers. Which is absurd.'

Rabbi Gershom is, perhaps, the voice of sanity in the karmic debate.

> What happens when you have a war and large numbers of people are killed at once, before what I would say is their normal lifespan? They die as children. They die in bombings. They die on the battlefield. When that happens, I think, things get a little mixed up ... When there's a war

it upsets the whole process in some way, and therefore I believe that some people do die too early, and there's unfinished business. They feel they need to come back. That's one reason why people have returned as non-Jews. Also, there were not enough bodies to come back as a Jew: there were not six million pregnant Jewish women, so they grabbed the first available embryo, regardless of what culture it may be, regardless of what family it was, and came back as fast as they could.

THE GERMAN PILOT REBORN IN SCOTLAND

I know of no Nazi leaders who have been reborn. Perhaps they have reincarnated in a South American safe haven. But I do know of a German fighter pilot who died at the controls of a Dornier aircraft and was reborn in Scotland … and joined the RAF.

Ken Llewelyn, who joined the RAF in the 1960s and trained as a pilot, had to leave when he found he had a fear of flying at high altitudes. He emigrated to Australia, where he became a senior public relations officer with the Royal Australian Air Force, and there he had a sitting with a medium who gave him a surprising message which explained his phobia. She told him he had been a German Luftwaffe pilot and had been shot down over England. On a visit to England soon afterwards, he visited the Arthur Findlay College, a Spiritualist centre at Stansted, Essex, and received further mediumistic messages about his alleged past life. These included the fact that he had been decapitated in the crash and that he would receive information from a relative that would be helpful.

He then travelled to Newport, Wales, where his uncle told him that, while on patrol duty at Sheringham, on the marshes of Norfolk, around 1942, 'he had actually picked up the headless body of a Dornier pilot still wearing all the Luftwaffe badges and insignias'. This information enabled Ken Llewelyn to identify the pilot as Friedrich Wilhelm Dorflinger. An insight into how the aircraft crashed came when Ken was hypnotically regressed and he relived the moment when the controls jammed, one of the engines caught fire and he told the crew to bail out.

The astonishing end to his eight-year past-life quest came when Ken Llewelyn tracked down Helmut Scrypezak – the man who was his co-pilot in his past life and the only survivor of the crash – and they were reunited. In his book, *Flight Into the Ages*, he says that at the end of their meeting 'we both threw our arms around each other with tears in our eyes'.

chapter sixteen

'I'M COMING BACK'

THE REBORN PRIEST

Dona Marine was startled to hear a man's voice calling her name in her empty Brazilian home and to see the curtains move in a strange way. Both experiences, she felt sure, were paranormal. She also felt sure she recognised the voice. It belonged to Father Jonathan, a priest who had been her school chaplain many years earlier, and with whom she had formed an intense but wholly innocent relationship which continued after her school days and marriage. It had ended only when he went to another town and Dona began raising a large family. But why, in 1972, many years after their parting, had she suddenly heard his voice?

What Dona Marine could not possibly have known by any normal means was that on that very day, 500 miles (800 kilometres) away, in the city of Belo Horizonte, Father Jonathan had been involved in a serious road accident and was in hospital in a coma from which he would not recover. That night she had a dream in which the priest appeared, calling her name and reaching his arms towards her.

What did it mean? Shortly afterwards the local radio carried news of the death of the popular, 47-year-old priest 'in a car crash'. The busy housewife was saddened, of course, and puzzled that her odd experience and dream had coincided with his death. But she soon put it out of her mind as she coped with more mundane matters.

In 1980 there was another addition to the family: a boy she named Kilden. She also gave him a second name – Alexandre – which was the one she had used privately for Father Jonathan when talking to him. The child's early years were comparatively normal, apart from the unusually agitated dreams he appeared to have, which were accompanied by minor poltergeist-like effects. But then, when he was just over two years old, he began to say strange and worrying things.

It all began when his mother called him by his first name and received the response: 'I'm not Kilden, silly. I'm Alexandre!' Dona Marine dismissed this as an expression of the child's preference for his second name rather than his first. But she soon realised there was more to it, for he added: 'I'm the priest. I'm Alexandre!'

His mother was bathing him, soon after his third birthday, when she asked him where he had come from – something she had liked to do with all her children over the years. 'And where did Mummy find this dear little fellow?' she enquired.

Kilden's response was immediate and positive: 'I was on my scooter and the truck came and hit me. I fell down and banged my head and I died. I went down there to the bottom and … and you found another me.'

Dona Marine tried to hide her astonishment.

'When did all this happen?' she asked.

'When I was Padre,' he replied without hesitation.

Showing remarkable composure, as well as an understanding of the needs of science, Dona Marine promptly dumped her half-dried son on the bed and went to write down his exact words while they were fresh in her mind.

All this happened eight years after Father Jonathan's death. But Dona Marine was surprised by Kilden's reference to a scooter: the radio report of Father Jonathan's death had said it was the result of a car crash. Dona Marine checked with the police and they provided her with a full report of the accident which showed that the priest *had* been riding a scooter at the time of the accident.

Other information about his memories of life as Father Jonathan slowly emerged. He spontaneously recognised photographs of his mother's school, declaring as he pointed to the picture (and speaking as if he were still Father Jonathan): 'I was here and Mummy was down there.' The sound of a popular song which the priest was particularly fond of made him burst into tears. He also identified two names his mother mentioned. And he often talked about 'When I was big'. Many of his memories related to the cause of his past-life death. Kilden showed signs of panic when he first heard an ambulance siren and, during a rather morbid family discussion on the worst way to die, he insisted that accidents were worst. As he said this, he held out his hands as if gripping a motorcycle's handlebars.

Kilden still retained some memories of his previous incarnation when he was thirteen, producing a description of his departure from physical life which is uncannily similar to numerous accounts of near-death experiences. On hearing his parents discuss what it must have been like for a family friend who had been killed in an accident, Kilden interrupted:

> This is how it is. The one who's had the accident arrives and they put him in a room full of equipment which the doctors switch on. They connect the instruments to your head and chest and try to save your life. Then the person floats to a corner of the ceiling and watches the doctors struggling to save him. Then a big hole like a funnel appears in a corner of the wall near me [sic], trying to suck me in ...

'You, or the accident victim?' asked his mother, noticing his sudden change to the use of the first person. He looked confused.

'Well, I suppose it was me. I saw my body, and the doctors trying to save me.'

Those present then discussed whether Kilden had seen a film dramatisation of a near-death experience on which he was basing his account, but the teenager was adamant that this was not the case:

> When you're sucked through the hole and along the tunnel, you see a very strong flash of light at the end of it. It was so bright that I had to turn away. It really was bright and the hole closed behind it, by the wall. At the same time, the doctors move the screen of a machine that has stopped. They've all stopped ...

A neighbour of Dona Marine's wrote to Hernani Guimaraes Andrade, the country's leading psychical researcher and founder of the Brazilian Institute for Psychobiophysical Research, telling him about what seemed to be a well-documented case of rebirth. Andrade, incidentally, is another of my magazine's international correspondents. He followed this up by asking Dona Marine for more details and was so impressed by the full report she supplied that he immediately drove 500 miles (800 kilometres) to interview her. Andrade, who has examined seventy-five cases of reincarnation in Brazil, regards this as the best and has written a book about it: *Renasceu Por Amor* (Reborn for Love), which is available only in Portuguese.

Author Guy Lyon Playfair, who speaks the language, reviewed the book for *Reincarnation International Magazine*, and paid tribute to the honesty of the principal witness, Dona Marine, who insisted on the use of pseudonyms for all the characters to protect her family and refused any form of payment. There was praise, too, for the stringent investigation standards of Andrade, whose work Playfair has featured in his own books, *The Flying Cow* and *The Indefinite Boundary*.

Playfair concludes:

> I have seldom come across such a persuasive case in any area of psychical research as the one described in this absorbing and unusual book, which is both a fascinating human interest story and an exemplary piece of field research.

'ANNOUNCING DREAMS'

One interpretation of Dona Marine's vivid dream on the day Father Jonathan had his fatal accident is that he was announcing his intention to return to her, or re-establish his relationship with her, and that he did so by being born as a son. This may seem far-fetched but dreams and other types of predictions are remarkably common in cases of rebirth. Indeed, some cultures embrace a belief in what are known as 'announcing dreams', in which the individual makes an appearance to reveal his or her intention to be reincarnated.

The Reborn Husband

Such an example, from India, concerns a young man who died of cholera at the age of nineteen, when his wife was two months pregnant. Shortly afterwards, Mamd Nandan Sayay appeared to his wife in a vivid dream and said he would be reborn as her son. As proof, he added, he would have a scar on his head and would not take her milk. Just as predicted, she gave birth to a son who had a one-inch-long scar on the back of his head and refused to take his mother's milk. Further confirmation came when he was five years old. Rather perplexed by the situation in which he found himself, he confided to his mother that he was her husband and that his grandparents were his parents.

The Reborn Son

An English couple who lost their first child while living in Malaya were convinced that he was born again to them. The mother, who went there as the bride of an engineer, gave birth to Philip Pryce Smith in October 1920 but he died a month after his fifth birthday, having been stricken with dysentery. The father sent his grief-stricken wife on a cruise to Burma to help her cope with her bereavement and she spent most of the time weeping and praying. Then she had a dream in which Philip put his arms around her neck and said, 'I am coming back to you, Mummy'. This was followed by another dream fourteen weeks after his death in which Philip said he would be coming back 'two months after Christmas, Mummy'. In February 1927 she gave birth to a son to whom, not surprisingly, she also gave the name Philip. And a stone was erected on the grave of the first Philip inscribed with these words: 'To the Glory of God and to the sweet memory of our dear son, Philip Pryce Smith. Born October 22, 1920. Died November 22, 1925. Reborn February 23, 1927. "God moves in a mysterious way His wonders to perform".'

THE REBORN MURDER VICTIM

There was no announcing dream to warn the parents of Malik Unlutaskiran that their son would be the reincarnation of someone else. But, two days after his birth in Adana, Turkey, his mother had a very strong dream in which her newborn baby insisted that his name be changed from Malik to Necip. His parents would have followed this request, except that there was already a Necip in the family and local superstition regarded such repetition as bringing bad luck. Instead, they changed his name to Necati.

As soon as he could talk, Necati began describing events in his former life, using terms, words and names that were unfamiliar to his family. Then he told of an attack which had brought his former incarnation, when he had been Necip Budak, to an end. In that life he had been married to Zehra and had fathered several children, he said. But he had argued with his best friend, Ahmed Renkli, over something trivial, and been slashed repeatedly in the dispute. He had crumpled to the floor in a pool of blood and died.

Most of these claims were corroborated later and, when he was taken to Nicep Budak's home, he identified his widow and named his children correctly – except the youngest child, a daughter, who had been born posthumously. He even pointed to a spot on his widow's thigh where he said he had cut her with a knife during a quarrel.

THE DAUGHTER WHO CAME BACK

Not all predictions of rebirth come from dreams. For example, the wife of Captain Florindo Batista had a waking vision in August 1905 in which she saw her daughter, Blanche, who had died three years earlier. 'Mummy, I am coming back,' she announced. At that point, Madame Batista was two months pregnant. When she gave birth to another daughter she also called her Blanche. During her brief life, the first Blanche had had a Swiss nurse, Maria, who used to sing her a French lullaby. Following the death of the little girl, it was forbidden in the house because of its painful associations – but the second Blanche suddenly began singing it … with a French accent. Asked by her mother who had taught it to her, she replied: 'I know it by myself.'

THE 'BARREN' WOMAN WHO BORE TWINS

A similar case, from Palermo, Sicily, concerns the daughter of physician Carmelo Samona. Alexandrina Samona had died of meningitis on 15 March 1910, and, following a previous miscarriage and operation, it was believed that Mrs Samona was incapable of conceiving again. Yet, three days after Alexandrina's death at the age of five she appeared in her mother's dream and told her to stop mourning. 'I have not left you for good,' she said, adding, 'I shall come back again, little.' This upset the mother, particularly as the dream was repeated three days later and was accompanied by a strange phenomenon: three loud knocks on the sitting room door when there was no one there.

Friends urged Mrs Samona to attend a seance where she received what appeared to be messages from her dead daughter confirming her intention to be reborn to her mother before Christmas and also claiming responsibility for the knocks on the door. Not only that, but the child also revealed that 'there is still another one inside you,' indicating that another spirit was also planning to be reborn at the same time, as her sister. All this occurred while Mrs Samona was under the impression that she could never have any more children and she viewed much of what was happening as either a deception or delusion. Above all, given her delicate state of health as far as pregnancy was concerned, it seemed highly unlikely that she could give birth to one child, let alone twins, of which there was no history in the family.

Yet, on 22 November 1910, Mrs Samona gave birth to twin daughters, one of whom she named Alexandrina and the other Maria-Pace. What is more, the second Alexandrina had distinct similarities to her dead sister, including enlarged veins in her left eye – hyperemia – and a growth behind the right ear. Dr Samona wrote a long account of these and other similarities between the two Alexandrinas, the most astonishing of which related to memories of the former life. One incident is worth recording in her father's words. It relates to the time when the second Alexandrina was ten years old:

Two years ago we were talking to our twin daughters of a proposed excursion to Monreale [where] we have an example of the finest Norman church in existence. Speaking of this project, my wife remarked to the children: 'When you go to Monreale you will see some sights such as you have never seen before.' At this Alexandrina interjected: 'But, Mother, I know Monreale, I have seen it already.' My wife remarked to me that the child had never been taken to that place, whereupon she broke in with: 'Oh yes, I went there. Don't you recall that there was a great church with a very large statue of a man, with his arms held open, on the roof? And don't you remember that we went there with a lady who had horns and that we met with some little red priests in the town?' Suddenly my wife remembered that the last time she went to Monreale she had gone there with little Alexandrina some months before her death, and that we had taken with us a lady of our acquaintance who had come up from the country for a medical consultation at Palermo, as she was suffering from disfiguring growths on her forehead, and also that just as we were going into the church we had met with a group of young Greek priests with blue robes decorated with red ornamentation. We also recalled that all these details had made a deep impression on our little daughter.

PROMISES TO BE REBORN

Even more astonishing in their implication are those cases which record individuals promising to be reincarnated before they die, suggesting that we can somehow govern how and where we are reborn.

The Two Marias
Maria Januaria de Oliveiro – known familiarly as Sinhaí – fell in love with two men both of whom failed to receive her father's approval. One of them committed suicide. Sinhaí became depressed, then physically ill, during which time she told a

family friend, Ida Lorenz, that she was frustrated with life and wanted to die. She said she wanted to be reborn as Ida's daughter and would prove her rebirth by talking about her previous life. She died at the age of twenty-eight on the following day but appears to have been reborn, just as she said she would, to the Lorenzes in Rio Grande do Sul, Brazil. She was given the name Maria. As she grew up she spoke about her previous life, giving her former name and much other information. Indeed, her father, a schoolteacher, took a keen interest in her memories and recorded that she had made 120 separate declarations and recognised many people known to Sinhaí. Much of what she told her parents was unknown to them and needed to be corroborated by others. The Lorenzes, it seems, had more than their fair share of reincarnation experiences, as readers will already be aware from Chapter Four.

The Man Reborn as His Niece's Son

From Alaska comes the case of Victor Vincent, an elderly Tlingit fisherman, who told his niece, Mrs Corliss Chotkin, Sr, that after his death he would be reborn as her son. He also forecast that she would recognise him by two scars from minor operations – one near the bridge of his nose and the other on his back – which he expected to be born with when he reincarnated. Some eighteen months after his death in the spring of 1946 she gave birth to a baby boy who was named after his father. Not only did Corliss Chotkin Jr have two birthmarks exactly where Victor Vincent had indicated but at the age of thirteen months, when his mother was trying to get him to repeat his name, he said to her, 'Don't you know who I am? I'm Kahkody.' This was Victor's tribal name. He later recognised a number of people known to Victor Vincent and provided other information which helped to corroborate the case.

The Man Reborn as His Own Grandson

A strikingly similar story from the same part of the world concerns another Alaskan fisherman, William George, who told his son, Reginald, that after his death he wanted to reincarnate. 'Listen to me carefully,' he would say. 'If there is anything in this idea of rebirth – rebirth in this world – I will come back and I will be *your* son.' Asked how he would recognise him, William George told his son that he would have two prominent moles – one on his left shoulder, the other on his forearm – just as he did in this life. He also gave his son a watch, saying, 'Keep this for me.' Reginald gave it to his wife Susan for safekeeping and she placed it in her jewellery box. A few days later William George went on a fishing expedition from which he never returned.

Almost exactly nine months later, on 5 May 1950, Susan George gave birth to a son with two prominent moles in exactly the positions his grandfather had predicted. He was named William George II. As he grew up he showed many remarkable similarities to his father's father, some of which could not be explained genetically. He treated his grandfather's sister as if she were his own sister and addressed his father's brothers and sister as his 'sons' and 'daughters'. And once, when looking into his mother's jewellery box, he spotted the timepiece left for safekeeping with his son Reginald. 'This is *my* watch!' he insisted.

With the passage of time, we are told, William George II has come to terms with the fact that he is apparently his own grandfather.

chapter seventeen

CONFRONTED BY THEIR MURDERERS

THE MURDERED MOTHER-IN-LAW

*F*rightened by the sight of a woman she had never seen before, Sunita Singh ran to her grandmother's side declaring, 'She will kill me again.' In fact, Sunita was so scared by the woman that her grandmother had no choice but to leave the gathering they were attending and take the child back home. Later, it became apparent that the woman who had scared her was the daughter-in-law of the person Sunita claimed to have been in her past life.

This story of a victim apparently meeting her murderer is told by Indian researcher Dr Satwant Pasricha in her book *Claims of Reincarnation*. And, perhaps because so many remembered past lives appear to have ended violently, it is by no means unique.

Sunita Singh was an only child, living in a village in District Mainpuri, Uttar Pradesh, and was just two-and-a-half when her grandmother took her to a meeting in a neighbouring village. By that time she had already told her parents that she had been murdered. But the sight of the woman she accused of the crime seems to have triggered her past-life memories and, as well as showing instant fear of being murdered again, Sunita also started providing more information about her previous incarnation.

Her previous daughter-in-law, she claimed, had hired 'goondas' (bandits) to murder her. Sunita even described her futile attempt to escape from them. The case of Sunita Singh provides us with only six verifiable statements, but Dr Pasricha was able to confirm that a woman called Ram Dulari had been murdered in March 1961 in a village some $1\frac{1}{4}$ miles (2 kilometres) away, and that a post mortem examination showed that she had been stabbed to death, just as Sunita had claimed. Her body was cremated immediately after the post mortem.

Sunita was not born until 1967, six years after the murder, and her parents discouraged her from talking about her memories of a previous life, partly through fear of losing her, we are told, and also because they were worried that, if she did, her past-life murderer might strike again. Throughout her childhood, it appears, Sunita would develop a fever whenever she saw the woman she accused of taking her life during her last incarnation. She also had a phobia about knives and darkness.

THE YOUNG HEIR WHO DISAPPEARED

Ravi Shankar Gupta was far more forthcoming about his murder. Between the ages of two and three he told his parents about his previous life, giving his father's name and trade, the names of his murderers, the place of the crime and other details of the life and death of Munna Prasad, who he claimed to be. And later in life, whenever he saw the two men he had named as his killers, he was filled with fear.

Munna, whose father Jageshwar Prasad was a barber in Kanauj, a city in the Chhipatti District of Uttar Pradesh, India, was just six years old when he was enticed away from where he was playing and viciously murdered with a knife or razor. His alleged murderers were neighbours – Jawahar, also a barber, and Chaturi, a washerman – who were seen with Munna on the day he disappeared. Chaturi later confessed to the murder and the boy's mutilated and severed head, and some of his clothes, were later found. But, after being officially charged with the murder, Chaturi withdrew his confession and, there being no witnesses to the crime, the case collapsed and both men were freed.

Their motive, it was alleged, was to rob Jageshwar Prasad of an heir so that one of the men, a relative, might inherit the property.

Ravi Shankar Gupta was born in July 1951, six months after Munna's killing, and first made his parents aware of his past-life memories by asking for toys which he claimed were in his 'other home'. Among those who testified to his statements about a previous existence, and particularly the murder, was his schoolteacher who heard them before Ravi Shankar reached the age of six.

Eventually, word reached Munna's father who visited the Gupta home, much to the annoyance of Ravi Shankar's father who regarded it as an intrusion and also feared that he might try to take his son away from him. He refused to talk to the visitor or to let Ravi Shankar do so. But his mother later permitted a meeting between the two at which the boy was able to give an account of the murder which corresponded very closely to what the murdered child's father had been able to put together, based on Chaturi's retracted confession and his own inspection of the murder site and the mutilated body. Ravi Shankar's father, however, refused to co-operate, beat the boy severely to stop him talking about his previous life, and even sent him away from the district for over a year.

In fact, Ravi Shankar Gupta's detailed account of Munna Prasad's murder and his identification of the alleged killers so impressed Munna's father that he wanted to renew the legal charges against the men. They had been released five years earlier because of lack of witnesses to the crime. But the father's desire to see justice done was frustrated, either because so much time had elapsed since the murder or because his son's testimony would not have been accepted in court. In the case of Ravi Shankar Gupta we also find a strong, and in the circumstances hardly surprising, phobia about barbers. And long after the memories of his life as Munna had totally faded, as they often do with the passing years, he still remained afraid of the two alleged murderers, even though he could no longer remember the origin of his fear.

FORGIVEN BUT NOT FORGOTTEN

Not all victims display fear. Gopal Gupta, the son of a petrol station manager in Delhi, born in August 1956, appears to have adopted a forgiving attitude – but perhaps that was because his killer had been his brother in his past life.

Gopal's account of his previous incarnation came flooding out in an extraordinary tirade, not long after he began to speak. His family were entertaining a guest and Gopal gave the visitor a glass of water. But when asked to remove the used glass he refused adamantly, saying: 'I won't pick it up. I am a Sharma.' He then proceeded to throw a tantrum, breaking several other glasses in the process.

The Guptas belonged to the Bania caste, which is on a lower level than the Sharmas, who are a sub-caste of Brahmins. Why should Gopal believe himself to be a Sharma and what had provoked such rude behaviour? His parents demanded an answer. To their astonishment he gave a long and detailed explanation.

He had another father in Mathura, he said, and also two brothers, one of whom had shot him. He had owned a company which produced medicines and even gave its name, Sukh Shancharak. In the life he was describing he had a large house with many servants to carry away used dishes and utensils. He added that he had quarrelled with his wife. Having listened to this incredible story, Gopal's mother wanted to take it no further. His father was largely indifferent, but he talked to other people about his son's claims, and confirmation of some of his statements was obtained. Then the sales manager of the Sukh Shancharak Company, which manufactures medicines at Mathura, heard of Gopal's memories and was impressed because they appeared to bear a remarkable resemblance to the life of his former employer, Shaktipal Sharma.

The company had been started by Kshetrapal Sharma, who became a millionaire, and subsequently left the business to two of his three sons, Vishwapal and Shaktipal. He disliked his youngest son, Brijendrapal, partly because he had married a Christian girl, and so he excluded him from the pharmaceutical inheritance. Shakitpal felt this was unfair and allowed Brijendrapal to participate in the business, having evolved a plan in which the position of manager rotated between the three of them. In time, however, the youngest son began demanding a greater share of the profits from his brothers and they also suspected him of fraud during his period as manager. The arguments which followed affected all of them and spilled over into their domestic lives. Eventually, it seems, Shaktipal decided to 'buy off' his brother. Wives in India often control considerable sums of the family's fortunes and so he asked his wife, Subhadra Devi, to provide the money. She refused and this seems to have made the situation worse.

Brijendrapal's hostility towards his brothers reached a climax on 24 May 1948, when he walked into the Sukh Shancharak Company's offices and, after a brief argument, shot at them. Shaktipal was hit in the chest by one of the bullets and died in hospital three days later. The brother who killed him was convicted of the murder and sentenced to life imprisonment. By the time the young Gopal Gupta was remembering his life as Shaktipal Sharma, Brijendrapal had been released on the grounds of being physically ill and their paths eventually crossed.

Before then, however, the dead man's widow, together with a sister and her son, had visited Delhi where Gopal had recognised them. The elder brother, Vishwapal, and his wife Satyawati were also recognised when they called at another time. Even though Gopal was apparently unable to clearly recognise Chandra Kumari Devi Shastri, one of Shaktipal's sisters, she and her husband invited the child and his family to the wedding of their son a month or two later. It was at the wedding reception that Gopal saw his murderer – the younger brother from his previous life.

He tried to draw the fact to his father's attention by making signs but S.P. Gupta was deep in conversation and paid no attention to him. However, Vishwapal Sharma's wife later testified that she had witnessed Gopal's reaction and heard him say to his father: 'That man who is disguised shot at me.' He had correctly identified Brijendrapal, quite spontaneously, and his former brother now had a beard (disguise). On the way home from the wedding, Gopal asked his father, 'Papa, did you see my brother?' When told he had not, the boy said he had pointed him out, adding, 'Papa – he looked like a thief – guilty.' This was seen to be a reference to the belief that before the murder Brijendrapal had also stolen money from the company. After that, the boy was keen to avoid meeting his murderer but showed neither fear nor a desire for revenge. He seemed prepared to forgive but not to forget.

On a visit to Mathura, Gopal walked around the house in which Shaktipal had lived, having correctly identified it as his. 'This is my living room,' he declared. Then, 'This is my bedroom.' He was scolded for touching a piano in the house, but the child responded forcefully: 'Why should I not touch it? It belongs to me.'

Gopal was also able to lead the way from the Dwarkadish Temple in Mathura to the Sukh Shancharak Company offices. His father tested his past-life knowledge by trying to mislead him and was told sternly by Gopal: 'Don't consider me a child. I know the way.' At the pharmaceutical company's premises he was also able to identify the correct location of the murderer and victim.

One of the most telling episodes in Gopal's past-life memories concerns Shaktipal's quarrel with his wife over giving money to Brijendrapal. Her refusal to do so had exacerbated the situation and it is likely that, as the reincarnation of Shaktipal, Gopal held her partly responsible for his death in his previous life. Whatever the reason, when Gopal first met Shaktipal's widow, Subhadra Devi Sharma, he refused to acknowledge her, saying, 'I do not have a wife.' Only after she had left did he admit, 'She was my wife.' Asked why he had not said so at the time, he explained that he was angry because he had asked her for money but she had not given it to him. When she learned of this statement by the young boy, Subhadra Devi Sharma fainted! Despite the very personal nature of this dispute, the elder brother Vishwapal gave permission to publish it because of its evidential nature. No one outside the family could have known about it. Gopal's lack of affection for Shaktipal's wife was also totally in character, for their marriage was not a happy one and the problems with his younger brother had clearly made matters worse.

Gopal impressed nearly all of the Sharma family with his knowledge of Shaktipal's life and death. In fact, he was even able to recognise Shaktipal in certain photographs where his face was obscured, because he could remember the picture being taken. This, and other evidence, reduced some family members to tears. After a while, Shaktipal's older sister found herself calling him 'Shakti', and Vishwapal was equally convinced.

No one, it seems, asked the murderer for his opinion.

THE REBORN FARMER WHO NAMED HIS MURDERER

A sensational murder in Turkey is the gruesome starting point of our next case study which, although it does not involve a meeting between the victim and murderer, does have some fascinating and unique features.

A prosperous vegetable farmer, Abit Süzülmüs, was called from his home in the Bey district of Adana on 31 January 1957, by an employee who said one of the animals was unwell. They went to the stable where Abit, who was in the prime of life, was struck on the head with a heavy black-smith's hammer and almost certainly died instantly. Some time afterwards, his heavily pregnant second wife, Sehide, went in search of her husband and was killed in the same way. The murderers took some jewellery from her body. The couple's two youngest children, Zihni and Ismet, were murdered on the same night when the assailants went to the Süzülmüs' home to rob it. Three other children managed to avoid their attention.

Eight months later, on 30 September, Mehmet Altinkilic and his wife Nebihe were blessed with another addition to their already large family – they had eighteen children in all – when Ismail was born. Within eighteen months, when he could scarcely walk and talk, the child began speaking of his life as Abit Süzülmüs. This happened when he was called by his name but denied he was Ismail. 'I am Abit,' he told his father (and from that moment on refused to respond to any other name – his father even having enrolled him in school under that name and eventually changing his name to Abit). 'I have two wives. One is called Hatice and the other Sehide.' Asked whether he had children, Ismail replied: 'Yes, Papa, Yes, yes. Gülseren, Zeki and Kikmet.' These, interestingly, were the ones who survived the horrific murder.

Later he named his other two children and correctly stated that they had also been murdered. The tiny child then said he was owed debts and gave the names of the three people concerned, adding, after complaining of the Süzülmüs family's poverty, that he hoped they would pay up. In fact, on the basis of Ismail's memories, two of Abit's creditors acknowledged their debt to the Süzülmüs family and Ismail agreed that Abit also owed someone money.

But it was his description of the murder which was so extraordinary. He named the man who had killed him – Ramazan – and told how he had been called from his house on the pretext of looking at a lame animal, then hit on the head with a hammer. He also knew that his second wife, who was in labour, had been killed, as well as two children.

As with many such cases, the 'other' family got to hear about the claim and various members came visiting out of curiosity and a desire to test the child's knowledge. Ismail was also taken to where Abit Süzülmüs had lived and was able to identify which of the two homes (one for each wife) was the scene of the attack. The result of these meetings was that two of the surviving children, Zeki and Kikmet, who he ran to greet and kiss the moment he first saw them, accepted that Ismail was the reincarnation of their father. Hatice Süzülmüs, Abit's first wife by whom he had been unable to have children (hence his decision to take a second wife), also accepted Ismail as her reincarnated husband. Investigator R. Bayer witnessed the meeting of Hatice and her apparently reincarnated husband. As she took Ismail in her arms, her eyes brimmed with tears and he noticed that tears were also running down Ismail's cheeks. In many ways, these emotions were as convincing as any words. They both accepted that Abit Süzülmüs had been reborn.

The story now took an unexpected turn. Almost a year to the day after Ismail was born, Adana tinsmith Kerim Bayri and his wife Cemile had a baby daughter, Cevriye. By the time she was one year old she was talking about the life she could remember – as Sehide Süzülmüs, Abit's young wife, who was one of the victims of the quadruple murder. In fact, the very first word she tried to speak sounded like 'Azu' and this eventually expanded to 'Ramazan killed'. She also gave a graphic description of the events leading up to the killing, saying that the murderers had taken her necklace. She added that the child she was expecting had been born after her death – confirmation of this came when her tomb was later opened and the baby was found to be partly extruded from the dead woman's uterus.

Cevriye also asked her family to call her Sehide, but met with greater resistance than Ismail.

Just as in the case of Ismail, news of the apparent rebirth of Sehide in the form of Cevriye Bayri soon reached the Süzülmüs and Altinkilic families. Not only did Abit Süzülmüs's family meet the child but both Zeki and Kikmet indicated that they believed her to be the reincarnation of their mother. Then Abit and Sehide, in the bodies of Ismail and Cevriye, also met and discussed their life together and their memories of the last, brutal day of their previous incarnation. They met several times and exchanged gifts, and Ismail even indicated his desire (at the age of ten) to marry her again when he was older. It was a prospect he still relished at the age of sixteen – but Cevriye (then aged fifteen) seemed less keen on the idea. She was now embarrassed to talk about her past-life memories on the not unreasonable basis that it would be immodest for a young unmarried girl to claim to have a husband.

Five people were arrested for the crimes. Two were released, one was sent to prison, and two – Ramazan and Mustafa – were hanged after a delayed trial, by which time Ismail was already talking about his life as Abit Süzülmüs. Although, in his life as Ismail, he had not encountered Ramazan, when news reached the Altinkilic household that he had been hanged, the young boy clapped his hands with joy.

THE MURDERER WHO ASKED TO MEET HIS REBORN VICTIM

The most extraordinary case of all, in my view, concerns Reena Gupta, who was less than two years old when she told her grandmother in New Delhi, 'I have a *gharwala* [husband]. My *gharwala* was a very bad man. He killed me.' She went on to talk of her own four children and to criticise her mother's cooking and the way she did household chores. Eventually, a colleague of her mother heard of a Sikh family in another part of Delhi, whose personal tragedy seemed to match Reena's memories, and she began making enquiries on their behalf. These led her to the home of Sardar Kishan Singh and his wife, the parents of Gurdeep Kaur who had been murdered, together with her brother, by her husband on 2 June 1961.

Intrigued by the woman's account, the Singhs decided to visit the Guptas and arrived while young Reena was sleeping. On waking and seeing them, she beamed with delight, declaring: 'They are my father and mother.' The next day they returned with Gurdeep's younger sister, Swarna. The moment Reena saw her she called her by her surname, Sarno. And when they left, and Swarna proffered a gift of two rupees, Reena protested, 'How can I take money from Sarno? She is younger than me.' (In India, only a person which is younger than the giver can accept a money gift. As far as Swarna was concerned, she was following the custom. But Reena saw her not as an older person but as her little sister.) Later Reena also met her four children from her previous life and was overjoyed with their reunion.

But why, you may wonder, do I regard this as such as extraordinary case? The reason is that, when it received widespread publicity, one person had good reason to be intrigued ... her past-life husband and murderer. Surjeet Singh, jailed for life for the double murder, had been freed after ten years for good behaviour and decided to pay Reena a visit. When she was told of his intention, her first reaction was 'He will kill me again.'

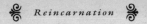

But she later relented. Joe Fisher, in his excellent *The Case for Reincarnation*, describes the encounter:

> When they met in 1975, Reena was nine years old and all the good behaviour in the world would not have been enough to allay her fears. Only with the greatest reluctance would she pose – perching nervously on the armrest of Surjeet Singh's chair – with the man she is convinced was her murderer. In fact, when Surjeet Singh tried to put his arms around her, she tore herself away.

TONGUE TIED

The Spanish Adventuress

What began as an experiment for Laurel Dilmen turned into a nightmare when one of the past lives she recalled under hypnosis began to dominate her life. The Chicago-born mother of two recounted an exciting and erotic love story, set in the sixteenth century, in which she was the leading character, Antonia Michaela Maria Ruiz de Prado. It was as compelling as any good, historic novel and it resulted in Laurel Dilmen comparing her present life with this earlier existence ... and finding it wanting. She began to neglect the people who mattered to her and to disregard activities in her present life because they seemed dull and worthless by comparison. Fortunately, she realised she needed help in order to restore balance to her life and she turned to hypnotherapist Linda Tarazi for help.

Both women had been members of the group at which Laurel Dilmen first volunteered to be regressed and so Linda Tarazi had witnessed her recollections of lives in tribal Africa, Sparta, ancient Egypt, sixteenth-century Spain and seven-teenth-century England. During a number of sessions the other lives were largely ignored and Laurel Dilmen's past-life memories focused on the colourful character of Antonia.

For several years Linda Tarazi had used hypnosis to relieve the suffering of neurotic and phobic people where other treatments had failed to help. She also took patients into past lives if they desired it. But she believed such 'previous personalities' were usually 'unverifiable and almost certainly derive from fantasy on the part of the subject'. She decided, therefore, that the best way of helping her patient was to collect information from Antonia, check its accuracy, and then demonstrate to Laurel Dilmen that it was fiction not fact. That would rid her of her fixation and restore her present life to normality.

What began, then, as a simple attempt to give the subject mental stability turned into a marathon exploration which produced remarkable results. Linda Tarazi reported on her exhaustive investigation in the *Journal of the American Society for Psychical Research* (October 1990). The three-year research project involved analysis of at least thirty-six formal hypnotic sessions and information which also came to Laurel Dilmen in dreams and flashbacks. Linda Tarazi spent much of her time in libraries and she also consulted historians and other experts who could throw light on the period in which Antonia claimed to live. The hypnotist even went to Spain to check out some of the claims.

Antonia's story is too long and complex to tell in depth here, but it is one of the most detailed I have read. The story starts with her birth on 15 November 1555, on a small, isolated plantation on the island of Hispaniola, the daughter of a Spanish father and a German mother. It moves to Germany – where her mother dies – then to Oxford, England, and on to Cuenca, Spain, where she hopes to be reunited with her father, who is now the owner and manager of an inn. On her arrival, however, she learns that he died ten days earlier. She struggles to make the inn a success whilst being spied upon by agents of the Spanish Inquisition. Three times she was summoned for questioning and once she was arrested, undergoing all the rigours of trial by inquisition.

At the age of twenty-nine Antonia lost her virginity when she was taken by force in the torture chamber. Linda Tarazi writes that it was:

a wildly erotic scene which aroused all of her passion and revealed her masochistic tendencies. She had secretly adored him [her torturer] before and now fell madly in love with him, became his mistress, and bore him a son. Her completely selfless love gradually changed his feelings from lustful self-indulgence to an all-consuming love for which no sacrifice was too great. They shared every faculty of mind, soul and body in a love that was both deeply spiritual and passionately erotic.

Antonia's life comes to a tragic, early end after a number of dangerous adventures with a cult of Satanists, a mission to Algiers, pirates in the Caribbean and a visit to Lima, Peru, where she meets her unknown uncle, Inquisitor Juan Ruiz de Prado. On the return journey, however, she drowns near a small Caribbean island and her lover almost dies in a vain attempt to save her.

It sounds like a Spanish version of *Indiana Jones* meets *Love Story* and it is understandable that anyone reading it would think it was simply a wild fantasy. The problem for sceptics, however, is that the account is replete with names and facts, most of which Linda Tarazi is satisfied could not have been known or discovered by Laurel Dilmen normally. After her 36-month investigation, Linda Tarazi comments: 'As far as I have been able to determine, all of the hundreds of detailed facts which formed such an intimate part of Antonia's "past life" are correct.'

Of these, she draws attention to between twenty-five and thirty highly specialised facts which were more difficult than others to verify:

Examples include: Date of the first publication of the Edict of Faith on the Island of Hispaniola; Spanish laws governing shipping to the Indies; types of ships used in the Mediterranean and the Atlantic, and details about them; dates and contents of the Spanish indexes of prohibited books and how they differed from the Roman Index; names of priests executed in England in 1581 and 1582, and the method of execution; and information about a college in Cuenca.

Nor were these facts volunteered by Antonia. They came in response to direct questions. In fact, from the beginning, Linda Tarazi observes, Laurel Dilmen (or Antonia):

seemed little concerned with facts, revealing them only when they were an essential part of her story. Never did she recite lists of facts such as monetary values, commodities, artifacts, etc., as we find in some 'past-life' tales. That she was well acquainted with this information was brought out only by intensive questioning ... [and] it became obvious that she probably knew many times as many facts as she bothered to volunteer in her narration.

The most astonishing aspect of the Antonia case, however, is that only someone with a knowledge of Spanish and plenty of time to research the most obscure reference books could have supplied all the information which was produced under hypnosis. Yet Laurel Dilmen had no knowledge of the language. Two of the facts she gave were at first denied by the authorities in Spain with whom Linda Tarazi checked. But Laurel Dilmen was proved right and they were wrong. Part of the hypnotist's intense research in this case involved her visiting Spain and checking through the Episcopal Archives.

Reincarnation researchers regard cases involving either 'responsive xenoglossy' or 'xenoglossy' as among the most evidential. The former means that a person who cannot normally speak another language is able to respond in that tongue to questions asked in that tongue. The latter is a knowledge of another language without being able to converse or respond to it. The Laurel Dilmen case falls into the second category.

'She pronounced Spanish names very well,' Linda Tarazi records:

recited the prayers required by the Inquisition in Latin, referred to special methods of making the sign of the cross, the *signo* and *santiguado*, unknown to most Spanish-speaking priests today, and composed words and music to a song in Latin, and music for the Latin *Pater Noster*, both of which she is recorded singing. But [Laurel Dilmen] exhibited little responsive xenoglossy in Spanish or Latin.

The hypnotist read books, watched films and interviewed her subject's family, friends and acquaintances over the first forty-five years of her life in a search for clues as to where her incredible knowledge of sixteenth-century Spain had come from. She found nothing. Remember that Linda Tarazi's aim was to prove her subject's memories to be false and in this she failed miserably. But she *was* able to rid Laurel Dilmen of her obsession with Antonia by getting her to fantasise under hypnosis about how that life could have had a happy ending if she had not drowned.

Laurel Dilmen is convinced that her memories are real and that she once lived the life of Antonia Michaela Maria Ruiz de Prado. Before reaching her own conclusion, Linda Tarazi sets out fourteen possible explanations for this remarkable hypnotic recall, dismissing most of them totally and leaving the door slightly open on just a couple. These include telepathic communication with a discarnate entity and a peculiar type of spirit possession. Reincarnation, she concludes, 'is the only one which, by itself, can account for the personality, feelings and attitudes of Antonia, as well as for all the obscure historical facts reported, simply and reasonably. Therefore, I tend to concur with Laurel Dilmen.'

Is this, then, one of the best cases for reincarnation? Possibly. But there is one flaw. Although all the other facts have checked out, so far no evidence has come to light to prove that anyone by the name of Antonia Michaela Maria Ruiz de Prado ever lived. But records have been found for all the other people she named in her story, including her lover.

SPEAKING ARCHAIC LANGUAGES

There are a number of other cases on record which involve the use of language, to varying degrees, and most of these have been produced under hypnosis. Glenn Ford, who made more films than most Hollywood actors, has recalled five lives under hypnosis, including one as Emile Langevin, an expert horseman in King Louis XIV's House Cavalry. While recalling this life, the veteran actor spoke French with ease. Hemendra Nath Banerjee, in his book *Americans Who Have Been Reincarnated*, says that Ford's normal French vocabulary is composed of a few haltingly spoken grammar-book phrases.

But experts at the University of California, Los Angeles, 'were very impressed' when they heard tape-recordings of his regression sessions. 'They said Ford was not only speaking French adeptly, but he was using the Parisian French of the 1670s.'

Incidentally, whilst recalling another life under hypnosis – that of Charles Stewart of Elgin, Scotland – Glenn Ford played Chopin, Beethoven and Mozart on a baby grand piano, though he could not play a note normally.

Dorothy Rainville of Sudbury, Ontario, Canada, manager in a chain of toy shops, found that she could speak French under hypnosis, too. She recalled the life of Alexandrine Poisson, daughter of Madame de Pompadour, the official mistress of King Louis XV of France. 'Under hypnosis,' Banerjee records, 'Dorothy could not only give intimate details about her life in France, but could also speak French, a language which she does not speak in her present life.' When she heard a tape-recording of her regression she said, 'I was stunned to hear myself talking in a combination of Parisian French and English, because I'm not lingual at all and can't speak French. I just couldn't believe my ears.' The experience satisfied her that she was the reincarnation of Alexandrine.

An Italian housewife, Maria Rossenelli, could not speak French, yet was able to recite in full Jeanne de la Platiere's 'Appeal to Posterity' in the original French. Her explanation? She believes she lived before as the author – who was guillotined in 1793.

Under hypnosis, a New Zealand housewife, Melva Drummond, is reported to have talked and sung in the Maori language … as it was spoken in the 1800s. An expert on Maori folklore was able to converse with her and he reported: 'Even a full-blooded Maori couldn't duplicate the behaviour we've just witnessed, nor talk and sing in that fashion. That's 150 years old!'

English teacher Margaret Baker appears to have been an eighteenth-century gypsy in a former life. During hypnotic regression in 1978 she recalled the life and death of horse dealer Tyzo Boswell who died in 1831 at the Horncastle Fair, Lincolnshire, after being struck by lightning. Speaking in coarse, guttural tones and using Romany words with which she was totally unfamiliar – such as 'motto' for drunk, 'mello' for dead, and 'chopping greis' meaning 'selling horses' – Margaret provided her 'gorgio' (non-gypsy) interviewer with a fascinating insight into Boswell's life and times. She even found his grave, at St Mary's Church, Tetford, which records that he was 'slain by lightening [sic]' on 5 August 1831.

MEMORIES OF GANDHI

At three months old, Therese Gay uttered her first word – 'Aroopa', which turned out to be Sanskrit rather than French. It means 'liberated from matter'. Then, within a year, the daughter of French parents, born near Paris in 1950, began speaking English, despite her mother's efforts to make her talk French. She called her father 'Daddy' and placed adjectives before the noun, as in English grammar. After a while, however, she began talking of 'Bapoo' – the name Mahatma Gandhi was given by his intimates – and while playing shops she gave the price of an article as 'three rupees'. It was never possible to identify who she had been in her past life, but her mother and others were satisfied that she had been connected with Gandhi, either in India or South Africa, where he had lived for some years.

SPEAKING UNLEARNED LANGUAGES

The wife of a Methodist minister in Gretna, Virginia, speaks German as she recalls her life as Gretchen under hypnosis. This past life came to light in 1970 after the Rev. Carroll E. Jay, who was a hypnotist as well as pastor of the Anderson Memorial United Methodist Church, heard his wife, Dolores, talking in her sleep – something she had never done in their thirty years of marriage. Intrigued by what he heard, and certain it was not a dream, he conducted some regression sessions at which Gretchen appeared and began speaking in German. Experts who heard the tape-recordings were satisfied that it *was* German but insisted that she must have learned the language or been exposed to it at some time for it to have been produced under hypnosis. This she denied.

The case is one of two featured by Professor Ian Stevenson in his book *Unlearned Language: New Studies in Xenoglossy*. This is a sequel to his earlier work, *Xenoglossy*, which recounted the experiences of a Philadelphia housewife, TE, who was hypnotised by her physician husband (both of whom wished to be anonymous). During regression 'she underwent a transformation to a male personality which called itself Jensen and which spoke and understood Swedish in an intelligible way. This personality,' Stevenson adds, 'was not merely reciting meaningless phrases: there was exchange of meaningful phrases with Swedish-speaking persons.'

This does not satisfy Sarah Grey Thomason of the University of Pittsburgh. Writing in *American Speech* (Winter 1984), a linguistic usage quarterly, she tackles the question, 'Do you remember your previous life's language in your present incarnation?' After giving some examples of apparent xenoglossy which had come her way, and finding them wanting, she turns her attention to Professor Stevenson's first book, explaining: 'The hypnotic subjects whose speech I studied produced fluent gibberish that seems to share several linguistic features with TE's "Swedish" and with the utterances of people who speak in tongues in a religious setting.' And she concludes: '... the available evidence does not support the claim that anyone has ever spoken a real human language without being previously exposed to it in a systematic way in his or her current life.'

I wonder what Sarah Grey Thomason thinks of the second and very unusual case in Professor Stevenson's second book on the subject?

CHANGING PERSONALITY AS WELL AS LANGUAGE

The parents of Uttara Huddar, a 32-year-old unmarried woman living in Maharashtra in the west central Indian state of Nagpur, were astonished one day in 1974 when their daughter began speaking in a language they did not recognise. Her personality had also changed and she called herself Sharada. This caused consternation in her village, and the family found it difficult to communicate with her until it was realised that she was apparently speaking Bengali. This was confirmed when Bengali speakers were brought to see the woman.

Dr Satwant Pasricha and Professor Ian Stevenson began investigating the case in June 1975 and placed great importance on establishing that Uttara Huddar had not learned or been exposed to Bengali normally. Later, after going back over Uttara Huddar's educational records, they found that she had taken a few lessons in Bengali *script*, whilst studying Sanskrit, but learned only enough to read a few words – not enough, in fact, to read complete sentences and certainly not sufficient for her to converse fluently in the language. In fact, they learned that even her teacher could not speak the language. Nevertheless, some critics believe this undermines the credibility of the case.

What makes this case so fascinating and perplexing is that, whereas most of those who claim past-life memories are children whose recall is often limited and who soon forget their previous incarnation, Uttara Huddar was an adult woman who 'became' another woman. But Sharada's arrival on the scene was not permanent, as in the case of Sumitra Singh in Sri Lanka (Chapter 11): she came for varying periods, ranging from one day to six weeks. Sometimes she would be Uttara Huddar when she went to bed at night and Sharada when she woke up next day. At other times she would experience a feeling of ants crawling on her head and shortly afterwards Sharada would appear.

The Bengali-speaking personality was totally unfamiliar with tools, instruments and appliances developed after the Industrial Revolution and at first took no part in household chores in Uttara Huddar's home. She gave a detailed account of her life, naming her parents and a maternal aunt and reporting that she had married at the age of seven. She had died, she said, at the age of twenty-two when bitten on her toe by a snake while picking flowers. All the evidence, including the Bengali words she used, pointed to Sharada having lived between 1810 and 1830 and the researchers were able to find a family of that name, and whose members would have had the same relationships with her as those she described. She had no idea where she had been since her death.

Since Sharada's first appearance in 1974, she and Uttara Huddar have shared the same body, but as each personality takes total control it is oblivious of the other's existence. There have been indications, however, that there might eventually be a merging of their personalities.

Without doubt, the case of Uttara Huddar is an important one, since it raises some intriguing questions. Is Sharada just a multiple personality – an aspect of Uttara Huddar's own mind? That seems unlikely because of her ability to speak Bengali. Which really leaves just two other possibilities. Either Sharada is a past-life memory of Uttara Huddar which 'takes over' her body. Or she is a Bengali-speaking spirit who attaches herself to Uttara Huddar at certain times.

Either way, the evidence suggests strongly that some form of life after death is the only satisfactory explanation for this and other cases in which memories of events and languages appear to have survived the body's physical destruction.

chapter nineteen

DIGGING UP THE PAST

THE ANCIENT CITY

Captain Arthur Flowerdew had been troubled by strange flashbacks and thoughts of a previous existence for most of his life. As a child he had visions of a pillared building hewn from black and pink rock. These impressions would come to him when he picked up a stone of matching colour in the garden, or saw a building with similar columns. Confused by these experiences, the young boy spoke to his father about them, believing that he must once have been taken to see such a building. But his father, thinking the claims were fantasy, dismissed them, saying, 'I don't want to hear another word about it.'

Unable to suppress his memories of this ancient city, Arthur Flowerdew followed his father's instructions and never spoke of them, except in later life to his wife and two other people. By then, he had become an engineer, joined the Army (remaining in England throughout his military service), married and had children, then become managing director of a garage in Norfolk, England.

It was not until he saw a TV documentary about Jordan that he was able to identify the place he remembered from his previous life. 'Look,' he called to his wife, who was in another room, 'that's my city. It actually exists and it's called Petra', as the screen filled with images of the rose-red city. Now a ruin, Petra was impregnable at the time he could remember it, for it could be approached by only one entrance: the Siq, a narrow chasm which twists and turns between cliffs 100 feet (30 metres) high.

Captain Flowerdew was certain that in his former life he was a dark-skinned Arab soldier who wore flowing robes with a hood and headband, and carried a spear with a wooden shaft and a bronze top. It was his job to help protect the city and he had been in charge of ten soldiers. In those days of active service as a captain, he and his men would ride into the desert on horseback and relieve unsuspecting passing Bedouins of their possessions, which were often great treasures. Those who refused to hand them over were killed instantly, he recalled. Petra was inhabited by an Arab tribe, the Nabateans, and its strategic position enabled them to become rich and powerful by commanding the trade routes from the East and from Arabia, and dealing in spices, silk and slaves. It was only when the Romans established new trade routes and took control in 106 AD that Petra's domination ended.

One day, when invaders tried to reach the city through the Siq, the captain and his contingent were ready to ambush them. The sun blinded the intruders and his men had little difficulty in overpowering and killing them as they emerged from the 10-foot (3-metre) wide passage. One of them, however, 'came upon me and, with his spear, dealt me a fatal blow in my chest,' Captain Flowerdew recalled. 'I well remember the thump, and then I had a terrific pain in my back. Then – nothing more.'

It was not until he saw the TV documentary that Captain Flowerdew began to think of his flashbacks and daydreams as reincarnation memories. If he really had lived at Petra, nearly 2,000 years ago, then perhaps his memories could be put to the test. Anglia TV, a regional company in the east of England, decided to find out and Captain Flowerdew, accompanied by BBC producer Douglas Salmon, a camera crew and leading archaeologist Professor Iain Browning, was flown to Amman and taken on to Petra in August 1978. The result was a fascinating half-hour TV documentary.

The first test was to see if Captain Flowerdew could find the Siq in an area with a circumferences of 30 miles (48 kilometres). 'Easy,' was the response of the man who, until that time, had never left England in this lifetime. 'Looking to the east of the rocky area about 180 miles (288 kilometres) from Amman and well into the desert, we must look for a large rock which looks like a volcano with the top cut off. Petra lies just beyond.' And so it was, following these instructions, that he again found himself facing the mighty city hewn from the rock. He also offered an explanation for steps which seemed to lead nowhere. Originally they had been part of an important temple, he remembered, and this was probably destroyed by an earthquake in 363 AD.

One aspect of the Petra ruins – row upon row of pigeonholes which created a honeycomb appearance on one of the walls – had long puzzled archaeologists. When asked about this he responded immediately, 'Oh, I can solve that problem,' and walked towards a small hill and a shoulder of rock which hid the structure. This, he said, was 'The Office of the Duty Roster' and the holes had been formed in three perpendicular sections representing 'On Duty in the City', 'Off Duty' and 'On Duty Outside the City'. 'Each of the 60 to 70 officers had a different-shaped stone tablet,' he added, 'which would be placed in the appropriate pigeonhole. In this way, the commanding officer would know exactly where to find any particular officer should he wish to do so.'

But he was puzzled by the magnificent amphitheatre. 'I don't remember that at all,' he said, as the camera recorded his comments. 'You wouldn't have done,' the TV crew told him. 'It was built by the Romans, long after you had died.'

Archaeologists are still interested in the beautiful, ancient city and perhaps in time they will uncover evidence for the tin and lead mines which Captain Flowerdew assures us were being worked in his day.

After all, it is not unreasonable to suggest that, if reincarnation is a fact, then past-life memories might provide us with important insights into our history.

RELICS OF THE ENGLISH CIVIL WAR

Another UK television company recently sent a film crew to Scotland with Peter Hulme, who believes he was a Cromwellian soldier in a past life, and made some surprising discoveries. Under hypnosis, Peter Hulme has described the life of John Rafael and, together with his brothers, Bob and Carl, has been able to verify much of what he remembered – and keeps me informed as their quest continues. For example, he provided me with a graphic account of a Civil War battle that raged around a castle on the banks of Loch Martenham, yet there are no local records of such a conflict. A seventeenth-century map, however, shows a 'Loch Martin' and 'Castle Martin' precisely where his past-life memories said they were, and – though the local inhabitants were totally unaware of it – the Hulmes found the castle ruins buried beneath undergrowth.

Central TV decided to take their investigations further and filmed the Hulmes returning to Scotland in an attempt to prove that a battle had taken place. They filmed Peter Hulme as he recalled his Cromwellian memories, both under hypnosis and while visiting the site, and this was broadcast as part of a *Tuesday Special* on reincarnation:

'The year that we attacked this fort was late 1649,' he said. 'I heard a cannon shot and there was so much shouting going on. Some of the soldiers ran across the causeway to escape. There were people firing from the fort ...'

A team with metal detectors were then shown wading in the loch's shallow waters as their spokesman, Scott Sibbald, explained: 'All of these signals are very strong and [the objects we are detecting] would be of considerable size. They are about 4 feet below the water and it's impossible to retrieve them, given the equipment we have.'

What are they? 'They are clearly not supermarket trolleys,' Bob Hulme laughs, 'so there's a very high possibility that they are relics of a Civil War battle.' He and his brothers are hoping to return to Scotland and uncover some of the objects with the help of others.

But, to return to the Central TV programme, the metal detectors had more success when they were asked to scour a 'dried-up ravine' in Scotland which Peter Hulme clearly remembered was a campsite for 500 men in 1646. Sure enough, despite the fact that there are no records to indicate that it was ever used for such a purpose, the searchers recovered, in the words of the TV commentator, 'a haul which included musket balls and relics typical of a Civil War encampment. Who could explain how they got there ... except Peter?'

The Hulme brothers continue to research this fascinating case and are turning up new information regularly in their quest to locate the grave of John Rafael and prove that he was once a Roundhead, as Peter Hulme maintains.

ANCIENT EGYPTIAN COMBS

Even further back in time, the everyday life of the Egyptians has been described in such incredible and life-like detail by Joan Grant that her novels immediately caught the public imagination. But after the success of her first book, *Winged Pharaoh*, the English author admitted that they were not really fiction at all: they were based on what she called 'far memory'. She was psychic and had the ability to 'tune in' to what she believed were her past incarnations. She began dictating *Winged Pharaoh* to her husband, Leslie, in 1936 after picking up a turquoise blue scarab beetle which a friend's brother had brought back from Egypt. This caused her to 'change level' subconsciously and hear the words of *Sekeeta* which she dictated to Leslie. There were 200 sessions in all before the book was complete.

'The funny thing is that it didn't come out in chronological order,' she said. 'But when we came to spread it all out on the floor, we found it fitted together perfectly and needed no rewriting.'

It was the story of Sekeeta, daughter of Pharaoh Za Atet, who became a priest-pharaoh herself 3,000 years ago, ruling Egypt with her brother. It was, said Joan Grant, set in the time of the First Egyptian Dynasty. Leslie Grant, who had trained to be a lawyer but decided on archaeology instead, was certain that his wife had got the period wrong because it seemed too advanced. It was, in his view, the Fifteenth Dynasty, and he would have based that opinion in part on her references to horses, silver and other everyday trappings of life which he and others assumed would not have been available to First Dynasty

Egyptians. He believed the invaders she described were Hyksos, not Zumas, and he was puzzled as to why she made no reference to the Pyramids.

But, according to Jean Overton Fuller in her *Joan Grant: Winged Pharaoh* (one of the Theosophical History Occasional Papers, Vol. II), Joan Grant was right. There *were* horses at that time – the Egyptians had taken them from the Zumas. There was also silver. And she was also correct to make no reference to the Pyramids because they had been built during the Third Dynasty.

In her book, Joan Grant – as Sekeeta – described the ivory combs she used in the temple:

> carved with my seal as a Winged Pharaoh, the hawk of the trained will upon the triumphant boat, above the wings of a Winged One; then, below this, my Horus name, Zat, written as a snake, next to the key of life and flanked by two rods of power, power wielded upon Earth and away from Earth.

Jean Overton Fuller was startled when she came across a line drawing which exactly fitted this description in Walter B. Emery's *Archaic Egypt*. Could she have copied it? Hardly: Joan Grant's book was published twenty-four years earlier.

Winged Pharaoh, I should add, is just one of several far-memory books written by Joan Grant which describe just a few of the forty previous lives she claimed to remember, many of which ended violently or tragically. They include another Egyptian life, 1,000 years later than Sekeeta; a wandering sixteenth-century Italian minstrel; a prostitute on the streets of France; a witch who was burned alive; an American Indian girl; a Greek runner; and an English woman, Lavinia, who died young after three years of paralysis caused by a fall from a horse.

During these many lives, she had once died at the guillotine, twice committed suicide, been killed by a spear through the eye during a joust, bled to death after ordering her Roman court physician to cut her wrists, and twice been bitten by snakes.

THE CONFEDERATE SOLDIER UNCOVERS HIS PAST

Sometimes, a past-life memory produces physical rather than academic evidence. In her astonishing account of group reincarnation *Mission to Millboro* (see Chapter 7), Dr Marge Rieder provides readers with tangible evidence to support what is otherwise a difficult concept to accept.

Joe Nazarowski, a private investigator, was one of fifty Lake Elsinore residents identified by her main subject, Maureen Williamson, as people who lived with her in Millboro in a past life when she was Becky. Joe, like many of the others, agreed to be hypnotised and his story confirmed what she had said. In his case, he recalled being a Confederate soldier, Charley, sent to Millboro as a secret agent to destroy a railway tunnel. What's more, he returned to Millboro in this life, found the tunnel and even pointed out the holes he had bored in 1864 with the intention of placing dynamite in them. Another man, Pat Greene, said there was a trap door above a hidden room in one of the houses he had seen in a photograph. Dr Rieder checked it out and he was absolutely right. She believes there's a lot more evidence to be unearthed at Millboro and is trying to raise funds to make this possible.

DEEDS FOUND AFTER 400 YEARS

Dr Hugh Pincott, a former honorary secretary of the Society for Psychical Research and a member of its hypnosis committee, has revealed a remarkable find which followed a regression session in which he was involved. In a lecture to the SPR he said: 'One amazing instance concerned a girl who, supposedly back 400 years, described a house where one of the rooms had been converted into an old chapel.' He and a colleague eventually located the house in Hampshire and found that the present owner knew that his conservatory had once been a chapel.

Dr Pincott continued:

What he was not aware of, which we were able to point out, was the presence of a hidden cupboard behind a panel. Knowing where it could be opened, we did so in the owner's presence. It contained the deeds of the house, kept there for nearly 400 years, and which the girl had told us about on tape.

AUSTRALIAN HOUSEWIFE DESCRIBES SCOTTISH BUILDING

Hypnotist Peter Ramster conducted a fascinating experiment with four Sydney housewives which was filmed and broadcast on television not only in Australia but around the world. Each recalled a past life in another part of the world which they were than taken to in order to record their feelings and to check out the facts. All the cases were impressive but that of Helen Pickering deserved special mention.

She recalled living in Aberdeen, Scotland, as James Archibald Burns who had been born in Dunbar in 1807. Helen was able to draw Aberdeen's Marshall College of Medicine as it was in Burns' day. It has since changed but the TV crew found the only man who could confirm its former appearance – local historian David Gordon, who has collected every plan and drawing from the college's earliest date. He was able to confirm the accuracy of her drawing which showed staircases and corridors that no longer exist. How she obtained such historical knowledge, he said, was 'inexplicable'. A visit to the county library in Blairgowrie, where Burns had established a successful medical practice, confirmed the other details of Helen Pickering's regression memories.

THE GIRL WHO DIED ON THE *TITANIC*

It may be thought that, after all that has been written about the sinking of the *Titanic*, it would be impossible to throw any new light on this dreadful maritime tragedy. But writer Monica O'Hara-Keeton believes she has. In *I Died on the Titanic* she recalls her life as Lucie Latymer, a young woman who was a baron's daughter and ran away on the huge liner with her boyfriend, under assumed names, to start a new life. Her fascinating story may not add to our knowledge of the disaster itself, but it's a fascinating detective story in which the author takes us through the various stages of her investigation, piecing together the jigsaw and finding an unexpected twist at the end. It is amusing to learn that Monica O'Hara-Keeton has no love for the spoilt brat she was in that former life.

What makes the *Titanic* story of particular interest is that the hypnotist who conducted the sessions was her husband, Joe Keeton, who has probably carried out more regressions than anyone else in the UK. The number is put at several thousand, and some of the evidence amassed has been documented in *Encounters with the Past*, which he co-authored with Peter Moss. Keeton believes inherited memory is the most likely explanation for past-life recall but his wife is satisfied that reincarnation best explains her *Titanic* experience.

THE HIDDEN MONEY

A Druse boy, Djebel el Alla, who recalled living as a rich man in Damascus, was able to take his astonished relatives to the house in which he said he had lived in that life. He was just five years old. The woman they found in the house was his wife, he claimed, and he provided a wealth of other evidence, all of which was found to be true. Then he revealed that he had hidden a precise sum of money in the cellar. He took the witnesses to the cellar, uncovered the money and counted out the exact amount.

THE BURIED TREASURE

I spent a couple of days in 1994 looking into an ever-deepening hole in Wales as an American guided diggers to where he believed they would find treasure he had buried there in the 1700s. Jim Bethe, a numismatist from Arizona, has recalled under hypnosis the life of a British soldier, Jonathan Seaman, married to a woman named Mary Merten. While stationed in India he acquired a small casket of jewels which he brought back to England and hid in Wales. And in this lifetime he has decided to recover them.

Jim and his wife Stella had already visited Wales and he had identified the place, when a British TV company read a story about him in *Reincarnation International Magazine* and decided to fly him back to the UK and help him dig for the treasure. I recommended Scottish hypnotist Tom Barlow to regress Jim Bethe for the TV cameras, so that they could capture some of the drama of his apparent past-life memories, and Tom soon had him talking about what he did with his treasure:

> I take it to Wales where I have a hiding place. I cross the pasture to the incline near the woods. There is a barnyard there, buildings ... I have me [sic] casket of jewels and I have grandfather's iron box that he gave me when he passed. There are three boxes of treasure here ... It is in a place where few people care to walk. It is in the pigsty. I am opening one of the double doors and squeezing in and walking down into the cave.

Both Jim Bethe and a dowser, Elizabeth Sulivan, independently pinpointed a clump of trees in Welsh parkland, where they were convinced the treasure lay buried. It seemed a most unlikely spot, for there was no indication that this particular spot in a wooded area had ever been anything but countryside. The dig began. I would like to report that Jim Bethe found his treasure but I cannot do so. What took us all by surprise, however, was the solid slab of concrete some 3 feet (1 metre) beneath the surface which prevented the first dig from going any deeper. Back we went a few days later and broke through, only to discover a brick-built archway and wall and water too deep to make it safe to excavate any further. It seems we had found his pigsty but not his treasure.

Are Jonathan Seaman's boxes still buried on a Welsh hillside or has someone found them during the three centuries that have elapsed since he hid them there? Jim Bethe tells me he is still determined to get to the bottom of the mystery ... and the water-logged hole in Wales whose precise location I have promised to keep a secret.

SCARRED FOR LIFE

THE BOY BORN WITH BULLET WOUNDS

The strange circular birth marks on Titu Singh's head when he was born puzzled his parents. But they were soon forgotten as his black hair grew, hiding them from sight. Titu, however, could not forget them, for they were the cause of his death in his previous incarnation. They were bullet wounds.

Nor were they the only evidence that he was reincarnated. Titu had very clear memories of that former life, when he was Suresh Verma, the owner of a radio, TV and video shop in Agra, with a wife named Uma and two children called Ronu and Sonu. From the age of two-and-a-half he had talked about his 'other family' and described vividly how he had been shot, his body cremated and his ashes scattered in the river.

'We didn't take him seriously at first,' says his father, 'but he behaved as if he wasn't part of this family. Titu is just an ordinary child but sometimes he says and does things that only adults do.'

Eventually, the family decided to test his claims and his elder brother travelled 8 miles (13 kilometres) from the village of Baad to the bustling city of Agra, northern India, famous the world over as the site of the massive, marble tomb, the Taj Mahal. It did not take him long to find a radio and TV shop called Suresh Radio and inside he found that the woman running it was named Uma. She was the widow of Suresh, who had been murdered exactly as Titu had described.

News that her dead husband had apparently been reborn came as something of a shock to the woman and brought memories flooding back of that dreadful day when 'I heard a noise from inside the house and went out thinking Suresh's car had back-fired. He didn't come out of the car. When I opened the door his body fell on me ... I let out a scream.'

But the possibility that he was now living in another body was difficult to grasp. 'I felt very odd,' she recalls, 'and wondered what to do. I talked it over with my parents-in-law and decided to visit the family the next morning.'

Titu Singh was washing at the tap when she and Suresh Verma's parents arrived unannounced and he immediately shouted that his 'other family' had arrived. They sat on the veranda and Titu asked Uma if she recognised him. She told him she did not. He then asked her about the children and whether she remembered a family outing to a fair in a neighbouring city, where he had bought her sweets. This revelation stunned her.

Later, Titu was taken to Agra to visit the shop he had owned in his previous life, but even then his elder brother put his knowledge to the test. He arranged for some neighbours' children to be playing with those of Suresh Verma when the Singh family arrived. It made no difference: Titu recognised Ronu and Sonu immediately from among the group. He then went into the shop and remarked on changes that had been made since his death.

The Titu Singh story was the subject of an excellent BBC TV *Forty Minutes* documentary which was screened in the UK in March 1990 and in which all the leading characters, including the six-year-old boy himself, were interviewed, using sub-titles to translate their words into English.

His mother, who has five other children all older than Titu, confided that she did not really mind him talking about his 'other' parents for she regarded them all as part of the same family. She explained:

Sometimes he goes moody and says he is 'homesick' and keeps wanting to go to Agra. Once he became so insistent that he rolled his clothes into a bundle and threatened to leave! Even now we find that Titu does not regard this home as his own. He insists that he won't be with us for long.

Titu's father, revealing that the boy often insists on being taken to his 'other home', remarked: 'I fear that as Titu gets older he might break all ties with us. We love him very much but, despite being educated, we are unable to understand his story.'

Suresh Verma's widow has no doubts about what has happened. 'I believe that Titu is my dead husband Suresh,' she told the TV crew. 'But he lives several miles away. I expect we'll keep meeting but beyond that what can I do.'

The murdered man's parents were also impressed with what they had seen and heard. Suresh's father said:

> I am virtually certain Titu is my dead son Suresh. He clings to us with affection. Once in the street he came across a former nanny. She thought Titu was one of Uma's sons. Titu got annoyed with her, saying, 'Don't you know who I am?' We talk to each other like father and son. But I don't encourage it too much as it upsets his real parents.

As for Titu, he remembers his murder vividly: 'I was coming home from work. He came running from the street corner.'

Who came running? Was he captured? Has he been sentenced for his crime? These questions were left unanswered by the TV documentary, perhaps for legal reasons, but they made up for that by providing positive evidence of the birthmarks which Titu and his family believe are the bullet wounds suffered by Suresh Verma. Barber's clippers were used to cut his hair and reveal the two strange marks which are in exactly the same position as those shown on Suresh Verma's autopsy report, caused by a bullet to the right temple. In fact, the entry wound of a bullet is always smaller than the exit wound, because the bullet leaves the body at a slower speed, causing more damage. The marks on Titu's head even correspond in size, as well as location, to the bullet wounds on Suresh Verma's body.

COINCIDENCE OR PROOF OF REINCARNATION?

If this was the only such case it would be reasonable to put it down to chance. But it is not. In fact, a surprisingly large number of reincarnation cases display some physical character-istic which seems to reflect an aspect of the previous life, often a violent incident and frequently the cause of death. There are so many cases of this type that Professor Ian Stevenson is working on a two-volume examination of the best of them, with a projected publication date of 1997. It is regarded by most researchers in the field as his most important contribu-tion to the reincarnation debate so far. He has already given us a glimpse of one or two of the case studies he will be publish-ing, together with some preliminary observations, in a scientific paper in the *Journal of the Society for Scientific Exploration*.

After pointing out that the causes of most birth defects or pigmented birthmarks – moles or nevi – are unknown, Stevenson reveals that one in three children who claim to remember past lives also have birth defects or birthmarks which they or adult informants attribute to wounds on the person whose life is remembered. From a pool of 895 case studies which were originally under scrutiny (though he has since investigated many more), there were 309 cases in which such marks or deformities coincided with wounds – usually fatal. He and his colleagues have been able to research 210 of these cases to the point where they can be included in his forthcoming book. The birth defects in such cases, inciden-tally, are usually of rare types.

In making his assessment, he looked for a correspondence of 1½ square inches (10 square centimetres) or less between wound and birth mark or defect. 'In fact, many of the birth-marks and wounds were much closer to the same location than this,' he claimed. 'In 43 of 49 cases in which a medical docu-ment (usually a post mortem report) was obtained, it confirmed the correspondence between wounds and birth-marks (or birth defects).' That's a concordance of 88 per cent.

Furthermore, Professor Stevenson's studies show that the case of Titu Singh is by no means unique. In nine out of fourteen cases of death by bullet, he has found that the birthmarks displayed coincided precisely in size and location with the entry and exit wounds on the deceased person's body. One of the cases studied by Professor Stevenson is remarkably similar to that of Titu Singh and concerns a Thai boy who recalls the life of a man who was shot in the head from behind. He puts the odds of two birthmarks corresponding to two wounds at one to 25,600.

RARE DEFORMITIES

Not all birthmarks are the results of malicious actions. A Burmese girl who remembered being her aunt was born with a long, vertical hypo-pigmented birthmark close to the midline of her lower chest and upper abdomen. This coincided with the surgical incision made during her aunt's surgery for congenital heart disease from which she died.

Another case involves a Turkish boy who was born with a shrunken and malformed ear and also under-development of the right side of the face. As well as this awful disfigurement, the boy remembered being a man who had been shot at point-blank range, dying six days later from wounds to the brain caused by particles that had penetrated the right side of his skull. Confirmation of this claim was obtained in the form of a hospital record.

One of the earliest investigated reincarnation cases, soon after the turn of the century, concerned a child named Sikh Lal who lived in Rishalpure, India, who was born without fingers on his right hand. When he could talk he told his parents he had been Kashi Ram who had been attacked by an enemy, Chottey Lal, who had cut off his fingers and shot him in the chest in 1908. The alleged murderer is said to have heard of his victim's rebirth and visited the boy, who recognised him in a crowd and called him his enemy and killer.

In more recent times, an Indian child born with almost no fingers on one hand remembered the life of another child who put his right hand into the blades of a fodder-chopping machine and lost his fingers. This birth deformity – unilateral brachydactyly – is extremely rare.

This reminds me of the case of Ranvir Singh, which we published in *Reincarnation International Magazine* in 1994. When I interviewed investigator Gaj Raj Singh Gaur during a visit to Delhi he showed me a picture of a three-year-old boy who was born in Basayi village, in the Etah district of India, with no right hand or forearm. The child recalls living as Idrish Ali, the servant of a landowner, Shafi Alam Namberdar of Garka, in the same district, whose right hand was severed in an accident with a fodder-cutting machine. What is surprising about this case is that the accident had happened to Idrish Ali twenty-five years before his death. In addition to the missing hand, Ranvir Singh also has a birthmark at the top of his buttocks which is said to coincide with a bullet wound suffered in his previous life when he was accidentally shot by police while hunting in the jungle.

ANOTHER MURDER VICTIM WHO RETURNED WITH BULLET WOUNDS

Another of the 100 or more cases of rebirth investigated by Gaj Raj Gaur is that of Gulson Kumar Sakena who was born in Vasantpur, Jaithra Etah, in November 1991. Gulson, the son of a tailor, Nand Kishore, was playing outside his father's shop when he saw two customers, named Rakesh and Mukesh, from the Barna district of Etah, arrive to collect clothes. The boy immediately became frightened and ran into the house to tell his mother: 'Those people killed me. Please hide me, otherwise they will kill me again.' Later, at his father's request, Gulson, who was just two years old, struggled to describe his past-life memories. Then he pointed at two places on his body – one on his right cheek, the other on the left side of his abdomen – where birthmarks were clearly visible.

The person he recalled being in his former life was Kanhkumar Pandey, whose elder brother, Gyan Singh, told Gaur how he'd met his death. He had been travelling to Etah by bus early one morning when two young men caught hold of him and shot him in front of several witnesses. The birthmarks on the boy coincided with the two bullet wounds.

Intriguingly, one of those who saw the body and the wounds was Gulson's own father. Could that sight have somehow affected him or been transmitted to his wife, producing the birthmarks in their child? It seems unlikely since Gulson was born *on the same day* that Kanhkumar Pandey was killed. Another physical correspondence between the murdered man and the child is that Gulson's complexion is very fair (as was Kanhkumar Pandey's), unlike his parents or his brothers.

BIRTHMARKS OR SCARS?

One of the most extraordinary cases of past-life recall associated with birthmarks is to be found in the records of the Buddhist World Mission in Rangoon. It records that a twelve-year-old houseboy of Southern Burmese origin, who came from a Christian family, was well built and physically sound apart from unusual malformations of his hands and feet. There were deep indentations along the heart line of both palms and others across one palm and forearm. His feet and calves were similarly disfigured by lines which ran parallel to one another. A surgeon said these marks could not be accounted for by pre-natal injury. Whenever attention was drawn to these disfigurements, his right arm would swell and he would suffer severe pain. So what had caused them?

As he was lying next to his mother one evening, he confided in her about his past-life memories. He had been a rich man in his previous incarnation and had hidden a lot of money and silver in three adjacent houses, where he lived alone. One night, robbers broke in and bound him with wire in a crouching position, before fleeing with his money and other valuables. He was undiscovered for several days, by which time the wires had cut deep into his body and he had suffered a long, painful, lingering death.

Straightforward cases of rebirth are difficult enough for many people to accept. Those which have these bizarre, added physical features challenge our understanding not only of the mechanics of reincarnation but also of the spiritual laws which are thought to govern our return to Earth in successive incarnations. Why should someone who lost a hand or fingers in one life be scarred in a similar way in the next existence? And why should a victim of a vicious attack carry the scars from one life to the next?

PUNISHED FOR MURDERING HIS WIFE?

The story of H.A. Wijeratne adds to the confusion, in some respects, but suggests that guilt for bad deeds might play a role in such physical marks or defects. Wijeratne was born with a deformity on the right side of his chest at Uggalkalteta, Sri Lanka, in 1947. His right arm was several inches shorter than his left and only half as thick. His fingers on that hand were also much smaller than normal, as well as being webbed together with skin. As soon as he could talk, at the age of two, he offered an explanation for this deformity. He had been born this way, he said, because that was the arm he had used to stab his wife in his previous life. It was a crime for which he had been punished, and the child gave a graphic description of his hanging with details – later shown to be correct – about incidents preceding his death. He then identified the person he had been in that life – the younger brother of his present-life father.

When the boy's mother challenged her husband about this, he admitted that he had had a married brother, Ratran Hami, who had stabbed his wife to death when she refused to return to their home after spending time with her parents. Ratran Hami had murdered Podi Menike on 14 October 1927. The trial had taken place in June 1928 and he was hanged a month later.

Shortly before he was executed, Ratran Hami told his brother that he would 'return' and that prediction seems to have been fulfilled, though it did not occur until more than eighteen years after his death.

Wijeratne clearly accepted that his withered arm was some form of punishment, or repayment of a karmic debt, for the murder he had committed in his previous incarnation. So, one would assume that the birth defect had a purpose –

to teach him a valuable lesson. If so, it seems not to have worked.

When asked what he would do if the same episode with his wife happened again, he gave the chilling response: 'I would probably kill her again!'

chapter twenty-one

INTO THE FUTURE

DOOM AND GLOOM

It is July 1998 and the world has turned upside down. Instead of sunshine blazing down on the Arizona landscape, Chet Snow is looking at a bleak desert, as a steady, chilly, drizzle drops from a nearly black sky. He has come outside to check the horses and, that task completed, he now hurries back to the ranch, cold and hungry. It's his birthday but he knows there will be no celebration.

This is not a scene from a gloomy futuristic movie but the recollection of a man experiencing 'progression therapy'. This and subsequent hypnotic glimpses of the future have convinced him that the Earth faces a major catastrophe which will probably be a polar shift or some other tilt of the planet's axis. Whether this will be just a movement of the Earth's crust, which will leave its molten core intact, or a major orbital movement, perhaps as the result of a collision or near-miss with a massive asteroid or comet, is not clear. Another explanation, of course, is that it could simply be the result of an over-active imagination fed on a diet of disaster movies and the predictions of famous prophets of doom.

But Chet Snow's is not a lone voice. In an experiment started by hypnotherapist Dr Helen Wambach in 1983, and which Chet Snow continued, following her death in 1985, 2,500 Americans were offered an opportunity to 'progress' hypnotically to a future lifetime. There were remarkable similarities in their experiences, suggesting that they *were* seeing the future, or at the very least were all being influenced by some other factors in a similar way.

By the time his book *Mass Dreams of the Future* was published in 1989, Chet Snow had made a name for himself as a respected hypnotherapist and had joined the Board of the Association for Past Life Research and Therapy (APART), of which Helen Wambach had been a founder. For three years from 1990 he was APART's president. He had also discovered that he had a rare quality when it came to being progressed. The vast majority of subjects who volunteered for the project found that some 'barrier' prevented them from seeing ahead to events in this life but they could, it seemed, travel in time to future lives. Chet Snow, on the other hand, could peer ahead at events in his current life.

'I was able to look forward in time and see some things which are already coming true in the mid-1990s,' he told me when I interviewed him for the magazine:

and these were published in the book ten years ago. Already the Yugoslavian situation is where it is, the Russians are looking much less nice – there's a real political difficulty there which could well come to the surface again, as I saw. The weather situation; the increasing volcanic and earthquake activity; all of which is put forward for the mid-nineties, with drugs, drought and floods all coming on top of the other, as it were, are leading to this period of great change.

Of course, there are always those who believe the current times are the worst in humanity's history. Crime figures always seem to be escalating. Natural disasters always seem to be claiming more lives. There's always something we can use to paint a gloomy picture – and, with so many predictions some have to be right. But even Chet Snow has a 'get out' clause which is, essentially, that if man mends his evil ways some of the upheavals that lurk in our immediate future may not happen. This suggests that some form of collective karmic responsibility for the planet exists whereby man's moral or perhaps ecological misdeeds will be punished by all manner of unspeakable calamities.

As for his own future, Chet Snow seems remarkably relaxed

about apparently being caught up in a self-fulfilling prophecy. When Helen Wambach progressed him to his birthday in July 1998 he was not living in Arizona – which was where he had seen himself in his previous progression. Yet that is precisely where he is now living 'through a whole series of circumstances connected with my work' rather than any desire to help the progression come true. But there's a difference. In his hypnotic vision he was alone, whereas he is now happily married. He attributes this change in his own future to 'spiritual maturity'.

A DRAMATIC DROP IN EARTH'S POPULATION

One prediction with which many of the subjects in the experiment agreed was that there would be a significant population drop over the next 150 years. Official statistics support a decline but not as drastic as that seen by the 'progressionists'.

Jenny Cockell, whose memory of a past life as Irish housewife Mary Sutton has made such a impact on readers around the world (Chapter Two), believes she has also seen her future ... and it lies in Nepal. In her book *Past Lives, Future Lives* she gives us glimpses of a future existence as Nadia, in a village set alongside a hillside in a mountainous area characterised by finely textured, reddish orange soil.

Just as she did with her Irish life in Malahide, she took out a map of the area and found herself drawn to the village of Kokuwa, midway between Mount Everest and the Indian border. As well as the 'future memories' which have come to her, she has also used hypnotist Jim Alexander to help her uncover more information.

She writes:

This experience of looking into the future had a different quality from remembering my past life as Mary. Those had been like any other memories; there was never anything strange about them. With this newer experience I felt that we were linked; I was living the feelings not so much as a memory, but as though I was in the past and two-year-old Nadia was remembering me from her life in the future, in the year 2040.

She also describes two other 'memories' of lives, one an impoverished one in the twenty-second century, in mainland Europe (possibly Poland), and the other in the twenty-third century when she is an American woman working as a technician for Unichem.

She doesn't warn us of polar shifts or changes in our planet's orbit, but she does agree with Helen Wambach's volunteers that there will be a drastic drop in the world's population, which she attributes to the effects of indiscriminate chemical usage getting into the food chain.

A NON-LINEAR VIEW OF TIME

Believing that a human mind can retrieve memories of a former life makes huge demands on our intellectual and spiritual understanding. To accept that we can also look into our own futures, either individually or collectively, surely requires an even greater leap of faith or the suspension of all our critical faculties. Unless, of course, we are misunderstanding the nature of time itself. Jenny Cockell, who has always had psychic flashes including premonitions, says that when she sees the future 'it is as though the mind exists simultaneously at two different points in time.'

Her son suggested the following explanation:

> We look at time from the present moment; we see the past behind us and the future ahead, and we think of ourselves existing in the now. But this linear view itself may limit our understanding of time and of the mind. Perhaps precognition involves a kind of telepathic link across time.

But such ideas are beyond the comprehension of most people who, whilst happy to indulge their fascination with having their fortune told, do not want to grapple with the complex workings of quantum theory or other suggestions about how we might be able to tune into the future.

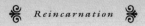

The problem with 'progressions' is that, for the most part, they are unprovable – at least in this life. But we should all be taking a keen interest in our planet's future and the impact we are having on it. After all, if reincarnation is a fact – for some or all of us – then it is we who will inherit the Earth and it will be us who have to sort out tomorrow the problems we are creating today.

chapter twenty-two

CONCLUSION

When Professor Ian Stevenson visited London towards the end of 1996 to lecture to the Society for Psychical Research, he admitted that, after over thirty years of intensive study of more than 2,500 reincarnation cases, he now realised he understood less about the subject than he thought he did when he started. There can be few scientific fields in which such a statement would ring true, particularly from someone who has devoted so much time and energy to investigating cases personally. But it does with reincarnation.

As we have seen from the numerous cases quoted, some definite patterns emerge from reports collected from around the world, yet they vanish completely in some cultures and yield very different results from the norm in others. Why?

In the majority of cases, a past-life memory emerges at a very early age and has been completely forgotten before a child reaches puberty. But there are exceptions to this rule, including some where recollection of a previous existence does not emerge completely until adulthood. Why?

In the majority of cases in which a person recalls a previous life, he or she is likely to have been reborn in a body of the same sex and in the same culture. There are many cases in which reincarnation occurs in the same village and even the same family. But there are other instances where very large distances separate the person who has these memories and the individual whose life is remembered; even cultural or religious differences are found in some of them. Why?

Most puzzling of all, perhaps, but at the same time probably the most convincing, are those cases – a surprisingly large percentage – in which birthmarks or birth defects show an uncanny correspondence with wounds or other features on the body of the person whose life is recalled. It would appear that, for some people at any rate, a brutal killing in a past life can result in the disfigurement caused by the method of death transferring itself to the new body on rebirth. Why?

I would like to be able to answer the question 'Why?' in all these instances but I confess I am unable to do so. There are plenty of theories, of course, but few hard facts to support them. Nevertheless, there are some aspects on which I can comment with greater certainty.

First, let me say that I have largely ignored the views of sceptics in this book. This is not because I disregard what they say. In fact, I read their views avidly and they make a valuable contribution to the debate. Despite their criticisms, however, I personally find the evidence for reincarnation compelling and I have endeavoured to give the reasons for this. I am, therefore, biased and this book reflects that. There are others who would put a very different interpretation on many of the cases I have quoted and it has to be said that even Professor Ian Stevenson, for all his efforts and with typical scientific caution, still makes no claim to have *proved* reincarnation. His cases, he says, are 'suggestive of reincarnation'. It is no secret, however, that reincarnation is his *preferred* explanation for the best cases and that's a view that I share. Only time will tell whether we ever reach the point at which reincarnation can be proved scientifically.

The major problem we have in assessing the evidence for reincarnation is that much of it, at least to start with, is anecdotal. We need to rely on the parents or relatives of children to recall what they said and we have to make allowances for their own beliefs, which might colour their recollections. Quite often, the investigators have to communicate with the families through interpreters and this is another area where the translator's personal bias might influence the way recollections are experienced. It is also wrong to assume that such bias is always in favour of reincarnation. Not all parents welcome the attention which is heaped on families with a child who has past-life memories. Some children are beaten or punished in order to silence them. So, researchers working in this field are faced with a very difficult task: they have to collect accurate information about statements made long before they arrive on the scene; sometimes they encounter conflicting statements and have to make difficult decisions about the witnesses' reliability and motives. This whole operation needs to be repeated, of course, with the family of the person whose life is being recalled.

The ideal case is one in which a researcher is notified of a child remembering a past life very soon after he or she first talks about it and is able to witness that recall and put questions to the child. Then, having gleaned enough information about the person who appears to have been reborn, the investigator can go in search of that individual's family, before any attempt has been made by non-scientists to contact them. Sometimes, such quests prove fruitful but just as often they fail.

Any scientist prepared to paddle in the murky waters of life-after-death in search of evidence that man is immortal can expect a rough ride from non-believers, and Professor Stevenson has endured many attacks during his career with stoicism and patience. The general thrust of such criticism is to question the quality of his investigative techniques and to suggest bias on his part.

English-born writer Ian Wilson, for example, in *All in the Mind*, criticised Professor Stevenson for using the services of Francis Story, an Englishman who was a Buddhist, and Dr Jamuna Prasad, an educational psychologist from the Uttar Pradesh district of India, who is a Hindu. He suggested that, since both are predisposed to spread a belief in reincarnation, they were not the best people for the Professor to use as research assistants or translators. He also argued that a 'difficulty' with Professor Stevenson's work was 'the absence among his published cases of any discernible rules that might govern the hypothetical existence of reincarnation'. He goes on to complain that they 'reveal no logical pattern' and elsewhere of 'alarmingly inconsistent patterns'.

The late D. Scott Rogo, an American writer and researcher who was himself critical of some of Professor Stevenson's work, was not impressed with such arguments. In *The Search for Yesterday* he mentions the review of Ian Wilson's book which he wrote for *Fate* magazine in which he dismissed the criticism of Story and Prasad because they were believers, arguing that Wilson could himself be accused of bias *against* reincarnation because he is a Roman Catholic convert. This, we are told, provoked an angry response from Wilson 'who obviously missed the point that I was playing his own game of foolish reasoning'.

In his own book, D. Scott Rogo gives an excellent summary of some of the criticisms that have been levelled against Professor Stevenson, and adds his own. He cites four well-known and often-quoted cases and alleges that Professor Stevenson 'led the witness' in the Mounzer Haïdar case (pp. 12–15); 'deletes important information when writing reports' in the Mallika case – namely that the father and grandfather of the child had publicly denied the claims being made for her behaviour; exaggerates an obfuscation in the Imad Elawar case 'to make the case fit the reincarnation mould without any procrustean limbs hanging out' (p. 92); and of playing down an 'important discrepancy' in the case of Uttara Huddar (pp.180–2).

These criticisms might seem trivial, D. Scott Rogo adds:

> but they indicate that a systematic bias may be pervading all of Stevenson's work ... The flaws in his handling of the Mallika and Uttara Huddar cases only came to light because I was able to cross-check his reports through my own contacts in India. The flaws that existed in his presentation of the Mounzer Haïdar and Imad Elawar cases are ones that only a careful scrutiny of the reports would reveal. So the question arises whether other flaws, omissions and camouflaging may be plaguing his published work in general.

An even stronger complaint has been made by Leonard Angel of Douglas College, New Westminster, Canada, who published his comments on the Imad Elawar case in his book *Enlightenment East & West*, and in an abbreviated form in *Skeptical Inquirer* (Fall 1994). He chose it, he says, because:

in this case alone Stevenson himself recorded the prior-to-verification memories, was present at the initial meetings between the boy who had the past-life memories and the surviving family members of the apparent past life, and conducted the verifications of the memories.

At the outset, the boy's parents 'believed that he was claiming to have been one Mahmoud Bouhamzy of Khriby who had a wife called Jamilah and who had been fatally injured by a truck after a quarrel with its driver'.

After criticising Professor Stevenson for not giving enough information about how the data was received, and precisely what the parents had said, Leonard Angel continues:

> Amazingly enough, the boy's memories are in the end held to be good evidence for reincarnation in spite of the fact that the best past-life candidate Stevenson found was not named Mahmound Bouhamzy, did not have a wife named Jamilah, and did not die as a result of an accident at all, let alone one that followed a quarrel with the driver.

These differences, I should point out, are very obvious to the readers of Professor Stevenson's *Twenty Cases Suggestive of Reincarnation* in which he deals with this very complicated case in depth. And Professor Stevenson's friends persuaded him to depart from his 'policy of ignoring criticisms published in magazines' and answer these points, insisting at the end that, despite Leonard Angel's views, he still regards it as 'one of the strongest' cases he has encountered, though others have come to light since he investigated it in the 1960s which are 'as good or stronger'. He insists that Imad never said the fatal truck accident happened to him: he merely described it vividly. And he refers to the possibility of a 'fusion of images in Imad's mind of "memories" related to Ibrahim's illness and the fatal accident of his friend Said'.

Those readers interested in what the sceptics have to say about the subject should also consult Paul Edwards' *Reincarnation: A Critical Examination*, even though its author clearly refuses to accept any possibility of surviving death and is therefore dismissive of evidence which points in that direction.

But Professor Stevenson is not alone in investigating reincarnation cases. There are a number of researchers who have replicated his studies and detected the same patterns and similarities. Among them is Professor Erlendur Haraldsson who, in 1995, published in *The Journal of Nervous and Mental Disease* (**Vol. 183**, No. 7) the results of a study he had conducted in Sri Lanka with twenty-three children who remembered past lives. He discovered that, compared with a control sample, they had greater verbal skills and better memories than their peers, performed much better in school, and were more socially active, but were not more suggestible. They were, however, more argumentative, talkative and perfectionist than other children. Professor Haraldsson promises further exploration to help us understand the significance of these findings.

I have already commented on author Ian Wilson's complaint of 'alarmingly inconsistent patterns' in reincarnation case studies, particularly between one culture and another. 'Almost all Tlingit Alaskan Indian cases, for instance, purportedly reincarnate with the same family,' he points out, 'while almost all Asian Indian cases outside it.' But such inconsistencies could be patterns in themselves and be a *strength* rather than a weakness. Stevenson, himself, has commented on these surprising differences. It seems that if your culture teaches you that you reincarnate immediately after you die, that is what will happen. If the belief that is prevalent is that you will be reborn in your family, that is also what will happen. If you have been taught that your soul will be reborn within two years of death, that is also what will occur. Culture, belief and even the individual's desires appear to dictate when, where and to whom rebirth will happen. Which prompts Professor Stevenson to ask, 'So what happens to people who do not believe they will be reborn?'

Having investigated more than 2,500 cases and written about a couple of hundred of these, it is almost inevitable that critics will find one or two of Professor Stevenson's cases which do not satisfy them. Even if it can be shown that every single case reported by the Professor and his colleagues is flawed in some way, that does not mean that the cases themselves are not evidence for reincarnation. The criticism is usually against the scientific method rather than the evidence itself.

More people than ever now believe in reincarnation, though I have to say that the vast majority do so for reasons that do not stand up to critical examination. As far as the scientific establishment is concerned, despite the valiant efforts of Professor Stevenson and his colleagues, we are still a long way from having enough case studies of good enough quality to provide convincing proof.

But neither fact precludes us from making our own judgements based on the evidence that is available, our own instincts, the spiritual insights we have, or the religious teachings we accept. I personally believe that some form of reincarnation does occur, for the majority of people, but that its mechanics are far too complex for us to even begin to understand. I also believe that if more people were open to this possibility it might help us explore and possibly shed valuable light on some puzzling aspects of human behaviour.

For example, in cases of gender identity confusion, it could assist individuals suffering from this condition if those helping them could accept that they *might* have lived in a body of the opposite sex in a previous life and have retained a memory of this.

Those psychologists and therapists battling over child abuse accusations and so-called false memory syndrome might also consider whether such complaints – often patently false – have not been implanted by the therapist but are 'seeping through' from a previous life in which parental abuse *did* take place.

And, above all, perhaps we could instil a greater sense of compassion in those who display racial, religious or sexual hatred, by convincing them that one day they may be reborn as someone whose colour, belief or gender they despise in this life.

In the end, reincarnation is not about case studies, academic analysis, statistics, patterns, facts and figures. It is about people – you and me. It is about contemplating the possibility that the life we are currently living is but one of many. It suggests that we each have an immortal element, a divine spark, an indestructible soul, which survives bodily death, and it follows that we each have a purpose in life.

If just one of the case studies quoted in this book has satisfied you that an individual has lived more lives than one, then that opens the door to the possibility that reincarnation is a universal law which embraces everyone. It is for you and I to decide what effect that realisation will have on the rest of our lives … and those we can look forward to living in the future.

BIBLIOGRAPHY

Andrade, Hernani Guimaraes, *Renasceu Por Amor*, (IBPP Monograph No. 7 – Portuguese)

Angel, Leonard, *Enlightenment East & West*, New York, SUNY, 1994

Banerjee, Hemendra Nath, *Americans Who Have Been Reincarnated*, New York, Macmillan Publishing Co., 1980

Bernstein, Morey, *The Search For Bridey Murphy*, New York, Doubleday, 1956

Carpenter, Sue, *Past Lives: True Stories Of Reincarnation*, London, Virgin Books, 1995

Christie-Murray, David, *Reincarnation: Ancient Beliefs And Modern Evidence*, David & Charles (Publishers), 1981

Cockell, Jenny, *Yesterday's Children*, London, Piatkus Books, 1993

Past Lives, Future Lives, London, Piatkus Books, 1996

Cott, Jonathan, *The Search For Omm Sety*, London, Rider, 1987

Cunningham, Janet, *A Tribe Returned*, California, Deep Forest Press, 1994

Dowding, Air Chief Marshall, *Many Mansions*, London, 1943

Lychgate: The Entrance To The Path, London, 1945

Ebon, Martin (ed), *Reincarnation In The Twentieth Century*, New York, The World Publishing Co, 1969

Edwards, Paul, *Reincarnation: A Critical Examination*, New York, Prometheus Books, 1996

Everett, Lee, *Celebrity Regressions*, London, W. Foulsham &
Co., 1996

Fisher, Joe, *The Case For Reincarnation*, London, Granada
Publishing, 1985

Gershom, Rabbi Yonassan, *Beyond The Ashes*, Virginia Beach,
ARE Press, 1992
From Ashes To Healing, Virginia Beach, ARE Press, 1996
Grant, Joan, *Winged Pharaoh*, London, 1937
Guirdham, Arthur, *The Cathars And Reincarnation*, London,
Neville Spearman, 1970;
We Are One Another, London, Neville Spearman, 1974
The Lake And The Castle, London, C.W. Daniel, 1976

Harris, Melvin, *Sorry, You've Been Duped!*, London,
Weidenfeld & Nicholson, 1986

Iverson, Jeffrey, *More Lives Than One*, Souvenir Press, 1976
In Search Of The Dead, London, BBC Books, 1992

Keeton, Joe and Moss, Peter, *Encounters With The Past*,
Sidgwick & Jackson, 1979

Llewelyn, Ken, *Flight Into The Ages*, New South Wales,
Felspin, 1991
Lucas, Winafred Blake (ed), *Regression Therapy, A Handbook
For Professionals, Vols I & II,* California, Deep Forest Press,
1993

O'Hara-Keeton, Monica, *I Died On The Titanic,* Birkenhead,
Countryvise, 1996
Ostrander, Sheila and Schroeder, Lynn, *Psychic Discoveries
Behind The Iron Curtain*, New Jersey, Prentice-Hall, 1970

Pasricha, Satwant, *Claims Of Reincarnation: An Empirical
Study Of Cases In India,* New Delhi, Harman Publishing
House, 1990

Playfair, Guy Lyon, *The Flying Cow*, London, Souvenir Press, 1975
  The Indefinite Boundary, London, Souvenir Press, 1976

Rieder, Marge, *Mission To Millboro*, Nevada City, Blue Dolphin Publishing, 1993
Rogo, D. Scott, *The Search For Yesterday*, New Jersey, Prentice-Hall, 1985

Sandweiss, Dr Samuel, *Sai Baba … The Holy Man And The Psychiatrist*, San Diego, Birth Day Publishing Company, 1975
Snow, Chet, *Mass Dreams Of The Future*, London, Aquarian Press, 1991
Stearn, Jess, *Yoga, Youth and Reincarnation*, New York, Doubleday, 1965
  Edgar Cayce: The Sleeping Prophet, New York, Doubleday, 1967
  Soulmates, New York, Bantam Books, 1984.
Stevenson, Ian, *Twenty Cases Suggestive Of Reincarnation*, Charlottesville, University Press of Virginia, 1974 [First published as Vol 26, 1966, of the *Proceedings* of the American Society for Psychical Research]
  Xenoglossy: A Review And Report Of A Case, Bristol, John Wright & Sons, 1974 [First published as Vol 31 of the *Proceedings* of the American Society for Psychical Research]
  Cases Of The Reincarnation Type, Vol 1, Ten Cases In India, Charlottesville, University Press of Virginia, 1975
  Cases Of The Reincarnation Type, Vol 2, Ten Cases In Sri Lanka, Charlottesville, University Press of Virginia, 1977
  Cases Of The Reincarnation Type, Vol 3, Twelve Cases In Lebanon and Turkey, Charlottesville, University Press of Virginia, 1980
  Cases Of The Reincarnation Type, Vol 4, Twelve Cases In Thailand and Burma, Charlottesville, University Press of Virginia, 1983
  Unlearned Language: new studies In Xenoglossy Charlottesville, University Press of Virginia, 1984

Children Who Remember Previous Lives Charlottesville, University Press of Virginia, 1987

Sutphen, Dick, *Earthly Purpose,* New York, Pocket Books, 1990

Weiss, Brian, *Many Lives, Many Masters,* London, Piatkus Books, 1994

Only Love Is Real, London, Piatkus Books, 1996

Whitton, Joel L and Fisher, Joe, *Life Between Life,* London, Grafton Books, 1986

Wilson, Ian, *Mind Out Of Time,* London, Victor Gollancz, 1981

Woolger, Dr Roger, *Other Lives, Other Selves*, New York, Bantam Books, 1988

INDEX

REINCARNATION INTERNATIONAL MAGAZINE

is available on subscription. For details
contact:
P.O. Box 10839
London
SW13 0ZG
Tel and fax: 0181-241 2184

e-mail: reincarn@dircon.co.uk
Web site: http://www.dircon.co.uk/reincarn/

The author would like to hear of new case studies
which those concerned believe have been
satisfactorily verified

PIATKUS BOOKS

If you have enjoyed reading this book, you may be interested in other titles published by Piatkus. These include:

The Afterlife: An investigation into the mysteries of life after death   Jenny Randles and Peter Hough

As I See It: A psychic's guide to developing your healing and sensing abilities   Betty F. Balcombe

Ask Your Angels: A practical guide to working with angels to enrich your life   Alma Daniel, Timothy Wyllie and Andrew Ramer

At Peace In The Light: A man who died twice reveals amazing insights into life, death and its mysteries   Dannion Brinkley with Paul Perry

Beyond Belief: How to develop mystical consciousness and discover the God within   Peter Spink

Care Of The Soul: How to add depth and meaning to your everyday life   Thomas Moore

Child Of Eternity, A: An extraordinary young girl's message from the world beyond   Adriana Rocha and Kristi Jorde

Complete Book Of UFOs, The: An investigation into alien contacts and encounters   Peter Hough and Jenny Randles

Complete Healer, The: How to awaken and develop your healing potential   David Furlong

Contacting The Spirit World: How to develop your psychic abilities and stay in touch with loved ones   Linda Williamson

Energy Connection, The: Answers to life's important questions   Betty F. Balcombe

Handbook For The Soul: A collection of writings from over 30 celebrated spiritual writers   Richard Clarkson and Benjamin Shields (eds.)

Healing Breakthroughs: How your attitudes and beliefs can affect your health   Dr Larry Dossey

Healing Experience, The: Remarkable cases from a professional healer   Malcolm S Southwood

Hymns To An Unknown God: Awakening the spirit in everyday life   Sam Keen

I Ching or Book Of Changes, The: A guide to life's turning points   Brian Browne Walker

Journeys Through Time: A guide to reincarnation and your immortal soul   Soozi Holbeche

Karma And Reincarnation: The key to spiritual evolution and enlightenment   Dr Hiroshi Motoyama

Lao Tzu's Tao Te Ching   Timothy Freke

Life After Death And The World Beyond: Investigating heaven and the spiritual dimension   Jenny Randles and Peter Hough

Life Signs: An astrological guide to the way we live   Julia and Derek Parker

Living Magically: A new vision of reality   Gill Edwards

Many Lives, Many Masters: The true story of a prominent psychiatrist, his young patient and the past-life therapy that changed both of their lives   Dr Brian L. Weiss

Mary's Message To The World   Annie Kirkwood

Message Of Love, A: A channelled guide to our future   Ruth White

Miracles: A collection of true stories which prove that miracles do happen   Cassandra Eason

For a free brochure with information on our full range of titles, please write to:

Piatkus Books
Freepost 7 (WD 4505)
London W1E 4EZ

PIATKUS